P9-CCL-542

You Are Born to Fly

Where do our e-mails come from?

You Are Born to Fly

An American Scholar Shares
Wit and Wisdom with
Young China and the World

Dr. Robert S. Herman

MP Momentum Publishers
Albany, New York

Copyright © 2010 Robert S. Herman

All Rights Reserved. Except as permitted under current legislation,
no part of this work may be photocopied, stored in a retrieval system,
published, performed in public, adapted, broadcast, transmitted,
recorded, or reproduced in any form or by any means,
without the prior permission of the copyright owner.

First published 2010
by Momentum Publishers
Albany, New York, USA

Typeset by Bookworm Composition Services

ISBN: 978-0-615-40485-1

This book is dedicated to
all the children in the world,
with the hope
that they will be able to learn
and to laugh together in a world
that is friendlier than the present one.

You are "born to fly," as you say, and there are so many ways of flying. I feel sure that you will find the one that suits you best and that your flight will end in happiness. I have enjoyed writing to you, and remember that the heart sees better than the eye.

—Respectfully yours, Bob

Contents

Note from the Publisher

Introducing Momentum Publishers: publishing relevant, results oriented books that promote the science of emotional well-being and the psychology of positive transformation. We are pleased to announce the first title in this series, Robert Herman's *You Are Born to Fly: An American Scholar Shares Wit and Wisdom with Young China and the World*. It is an historic exchange between a 90-year-old American educator and millions of young people who read and responded to his popular monthly columns in Chinese magazines. Through the mechanism of immediate global communication, Bob has forged a bond with a new generation of one of the world's oldest cultures, engaging the emerging Young China with the wit and wisdom of an "elder statesman."

In his emails, Bob shares his wisdom and his humor, counseling his correspondents to cultivate optimism, maximize their talents, and find fulfillment. Every day, from across the planet's most populous nation, high school seniors, secondary school and university teachers, Chinese English students, young women in love, job seekers, and exchange students, wrote to Bob asking for his advice. Sitting at his computer in Slingerlands, New York, Robert Herman, part Dr. Bob and part Confucius, demolished cultural gaps and demonstrated the universality of human experience, dealing with questions about family and teachers, heartbreak and true love, living and dying.

In one of her letters, a young Chinese woman named Kohli writes Bob about breaking up with her boyfriend and asks: "Am I born to fly freely, but alone?" Bob Herman replies: "You are born to fly and there are so many ways of flying. . . . Remember that the heart sees better than the eye." His advice comes in simple yet profound messages.

Seeing with the heart instead of the eye is just one of many compelling messages Bob shares with his young readers who write him every day from the other side of the world. His first book, *Adventures of the Mind* was written specifically for Chinese Readers. This volume, *You Are Born to Fly*, will appeal to readers around the world who will discover Bob's insights on the human condition and his vision of how to be the change we want to see in the world.

As a distinguished professor, public executive, international advisor, philosopher, poet and ping pong player, Bob is respected and beloved by a vast community of Chinese youth, as well as by an American community of admirers and fans of all ages.

Drs. Mary and John Valentis

About This Book

This book began as a series of columns published in two magazines in China: Overseas English and English Salon. These columns resulted from conversations with Ms. Mahya Zhang while playing ping pong in California in 2002. Chinese readers responded generously by sending me letters expressing their thoughts, their struggles, their ambitions, and their problems. This book is a collection of some of these letters and my responses to them.

The theme which pervaded these writings is that learning and laughter are the fellow travelers that we need on our journey through life. Our learning must give us the wisdom to settle controversies peaceably. Our ability to laugh together should help to relieve tensions, and create better fellowship. Humor can be useful in deflating arrogance especially if we can cultivate the gift of being able to laugh at ourselves. It is our hope that love and friendship and understanding will take the place of anger and hostility and violence.

Of course there will be frictions. Life is more than a land of peach blossoms. Our goal is to make these frictions fruitful, and to make them lead to the improvement of our world society. There will be tensions. These, too, can lead to greater creativity as they are resolved with good will, acceptance, and compassion.

Our earth planet is inhabited by people of different cultures, different histories and religions, different languages, and different life styles. Every person is an exception. No two people were created alike. Each of us is distinct and different, but we are all connected. We are all branches of the same tree. We all share the need for food, clothing, shelter and companionship. We all seek understanding and good will. We share a common hope for the survival of our global home.

War must be made obsolete. If we do not eliminate war, war will eliminate us. With the present and future state of technology, and the development of more horrible weapons, there can be no winners, only losers. We must turn our attention away from war preparation and shift it to peace preparation. It was Dwight D. Eisenhower who said that: "Every gun that is made, every warship launched, every rocket fired signifies a theft from those who hunger and are not fed, those who are cold and are not clothed."

We must strive for a world society where individuals give dignity and respect to other individuals, and where all nations give dignity and respect to all other nations. Our survival as a planet depends upon finding peaceful means of resolving conflicts, avoiding violence, and achieving both justice and mercy. Our greatest challenge is to find ways to reach global harmony between the poor and the wealthy, between the weak and the strong, between the yin and the yang.

The variety of cultures and histories in every part of the world are worth retaining. A homogenized world would be a dull place. We must learn to celebrate our differences, and not fight over them. I believe that life is a short interlude between two long solitudes. These two long solitudes are beyond our comprehension. It is this brief interlude, that we call "life," that we have some control over. My fervent hope is that by communicating with each other through these pages, all of us will enjoy this brief interlude as we learn and laugh together.

If this book has a purpose, it is to help create better understanding and better fellowship so this planet will be a better place for all of us to live and work on. If we can leave a legacy of greater tolerance and more kindness to others, and if we can be important in the lives of a few friends and neighbors, then our journey through life can be a success. Our possessions will not outlive us but the memories of our acts and deeds will.

If I were giving advice today to all these readers and to children everywhere, it would be: To act as if the future of the Universe depends on your actions. Only be doing this will we achieve the harmony and peace that this planet deserves.

I owe thanks to many. To Mahya Zhang for instigating these columns and to Overseas English and English Salon for publishing them. To my wife, Beatrice, for giving me the time to write, and for her loving support. To my sons Gerald and Arthur for their constant encouragement and advice, and to Dr. Zanvel Liff, the distinguished American psychotherapist, for his generous comments,

And my special thanks to Drs. Mary and John Valentis who dug through and edited volumes of letters to select those that appear in this book. It was Mary and John who proposed this book and made it possible. Without them, there would be no book.

I am grateful to all our readers in China, and especially to those who took the time to write to me. We cared for each other through our correspondence, and we shared many feelings and hopes and concerns.

And, finally, my thanks to Life, the supreme gift that each of us has been given.

Bob (Robert S. Herman, PhD)

Foreword

With China's own long tradition of wisdom teaching, it is interesting that a foreigner, an American from a different socio-political system, was invited to offer his personal views on topics of his choice in two English language periodicals.

The invitation to Dr. Robert S. Herman by China-born editor Mahya Zhang was an extraordinary choice. Bob had already been recognized in the United States in "Who's Who in America" as a distinguished university professor, author, and international consultant. Mahya soon recognized Bob's storehouse of information, knowledge and understanding as well as his passion to teach and to be helpful. He has repeatedly stated that his highest purpose is to be of help to others and to make this planet more habitable for human beings in every part of the earth.

With his global perspective, Bob is interested in breaking down barriers and building bridges. His mission is within the context of a deep respect for the separateness of ethnic, national and cultural identities. Among his other attributes, Bob can be described as a good-will ambassador promoting cross-cultural exchanges.

Bob has recently evolved into a soulful poet. He has an unusual ability to identify with the foibles and contradictions of the human condition. He often reminds me that we are all members of an immense family and must be bound together by love and friendship if our planet is to survive.

This collection of Bob's correspondence is a unique venture, especially in view of his generous invitation to ask for readers' responses and his offer to reply personally to selected letters. It is obvious to me that Bob's writings come to us through his mind but that they originate in his heart.

Never have I met anyone with such meaningful insights into every aspect of life. Bob has this uncommon ability to move outside himself and into the hearts and minds of other persons. He is an inspiration for all of us.

It is my hope that reading and rereading the treasures in this book will help broaden the understanding of its readers, and that Bob will be making a difference in many of his readers' lives.

Zanvel A. Liff, Ph.D.
Past President, Division of Psychoanalysis &
American Psychological Association

Correspondence

Togetherness

Dear Mr. Herman,

I am an avid reader of your column in *Overseas English*. I like the column very much, for it's your column that brings sunshine to my days and enriches my dull school life. Each time I read it, I feel a tinge of excitement.

You shared your poem "Nothings" with us. I am very interested in your poem, which is simple, yet beautiful without much ornament. Did you want to convey how important your friend is in your life? Being encouraged by the motto, "One who asks a question is a fool for five minutes; one who doesn't ask questions remains a fool forever," I dare to ask you to explain the poem. Your reply would be appreciated.

Sincerely yours, Ada (Shanghai)

▲

Dear Ada,

It was such a pleasure to receive and read your letter. My poem "Nothings" is a romantic poem. It was written to my wife at the time of our 50th wedding anniversary. It is meant to celebrate many years of marriage, and to express my feelings of gratitude for the togetherness that these 50 years have brought.

I am pleased that you enjoy reading my thoughts. If I can bring a bit of sunshine to one person such as you then all this writing becomes a joy.

With warmest regards, Bob

Beautiful Universe

Dear Bob,

Thank you for your beautiful article about your beautiful Universe. I was fascinated as soon as I read it.

You portray a society of equality, peace, justice, respect, dignity, and so on. We all dream of living in such a universe, but I want to know how we should live in such a universe.

Yours, Aisha

▲

Dear Aisha,

I am pleased that you agree with my thoughts on reconstructing our Universe. Of course this is wishful thinking, perhaps a dream of what this planet might be like. It is nice to be able to picture a world of peace and equality, and justice and mercy, and dignity and respect. This may be an impossible dream, but we were not born to accept the "impossible." I believe that when human relationships are concerned, everything is possible.

A popular novel written by an American author several years ago was titled "The World I Never Made." This always impressed me. The world we were born into is not the world that we made. We cannot be responsible for the world that we inherited from past generations. But we can be responsible for improving the world that we inherited. It is this responsibility which should be on every person's shoulders.

We are our brothers' keepers. We share the same Earth home. Each of us is born, lives, and dies. We all share the need for food and clothing and shelter. We all share the need for understanding and friendship. Why should it be impossible for us to also share the same dreams for a world that you and I have described? If enough of us can share this common dream of peace and equality, and justice and mercy, and dignity and respect for all, it will be the first step toward bringing such a dream into reality.

Please never stop believing that this dream world can be achieved. All it requires is that everyone on our planet agrees that it is a vision that is needed for the survival of our treasured earth home.

With warm regards and best wishes, Bob

Those Who Teach

Dr. Robert Herman,

This is my first time writing to you. I have read your articles in *Overseas English*. Your article is wonderful. I am a teacher in Beihua University. I just became a college teacher. I have gained a lot from your words, and I have shared it with my students. They said that your words give them encouragement.

To teach is not an easy thing, especially for a new teacher. I like to know something new. I will read your articles.

Yours sincerely, Amaly (Jilin)

▲

Dear Amaly,

I enjoyed reading your letter. I admire you for being a college teacher, and I feel privileged that you read my articles. I believe that teaching and nursing are our most treasured professions. They should be given more attention. The ability to help others is a treasured one. It is one that is badly needed in all societies.

Tomorrow's world will be built by today's young people. It is persons like you who have the responsibility for educating these young persons to build it better than it is now. I know very little about the educational processes in China. I hope they are keeping pace with the rapid development that is taking place in your country. One of the best investments any nation can make is in its educational institutions, all the way from early childhood education through the Universities.

I believe that it was Aristotle who said, "They who teach young people well are more to be honored than they who produce them." Again, I salute you for being in such an honored profession.

With warm wishes and best regards, Bob

True Love

Bob,

I love reading your articles. They give me a new view of things. Also, I want to know more about true love.

Thank you. Arnold (Mianyang, Sichuan)

▲

Dear Arnold,

I am pleased that you have a question concerning "true love." I have the same question. This is not a term that I use. How can there be "untrue love"? This would be a contradiction in terms. All love must be "true" or it would cease to be love.

Love is one of the most mysterious and confusing words we use in the English language. Maybe you can tell me how it is used in the Chinese language?

We do speak of "romantic love" which is the love between persons. This kind of love is glorified in our films and in our culture. It can be the source of great joy or great sorrow.

Love is not something we can keep for ourselves. It defines a relationship. Each of us has much love to give, and each of us desires to be loved.

To be able to love deeply is a gift. To be able to share our love with others is an even greater gift. To hurl our love in the wrong direction or to give it away casually can be tragic.

These are just a few observations that were stimulated by your brief note. I hope that there will be much love in your life, and that you will find others to share it with.

With warm regards and best wishes, Bob

Dear Bob,

I received your letter. Thanks! I am a high school senior. I like your column, not only your words but also the content, which lead me to the right way of life and help me out of darkness. You understand that I want to know more about "true love." Thank you!

Now I have another problem. Some of my friends, high school students, have puppy love, though our school does not allow us to. I was asked to have one too! We know that puppy love is not good for us. But how do we avoid this? Should we study with more of our energy? If we paid too much attention to puppy love, I don't think we would have a bright future, right? I hope you can give me advice on this.

Your constant reader, Arnold (Mianyang, Sichuan)

▲

Dear Arnold,

It has been many years since I experienced "puppy love," so I am no expert on this important subject. I am not familiar with the Chinese attitude toward young men and young women associating with each other as high school students. I suppose that the purpose of going to school is to increase your learning. Anything that interferes with this would not be desirable.

The question then becomes "learning for what?" I believe that learning about human relationships is very important. School should provide the foundation for our behavior in later life. Because all societies consist of the two genders, male and female, at some time it becomes important for these genders to understand each other. I am not certain at what age or under what circumstances this understanding should begin.

If "puppy love" interferes with your studies and makes you less able to compete for all the examinations that will be coming, maybe you better concentrate on your academic learning and postpone your romantic learning until after you have passed all these examinations. I wish I could be more helpful to you.

With warm regards and best wishes, Bob

Strangers

Dear Mr. Herman,

I have read your column, "Adventures of the Mind," in *Overseas English*. I like the column very much. At the beginning of your column you said, "I welcome responses from all readers," so I wrote this letter. Could I have a conversation with you?

I am a Chinese girl. Now I study in a high school. Next year I will go to college for further studies.

I want to ask you a question. If a stranger comes to ask you for help, what will you do? Maybe it is strange to ask this question.

Today I met a stranger who asked me to help him. He is a middle-aged man; he said his money had been stolen at the railway, so he had no money to go home. Because he was only a traveler in my town, he had to ask passers-by to help him.

Some people pretended not to hear what he said and went by him quickly. At first, I thought he was a swindler. But then I saw his eyes I believed he did not tell lies, because his eyes were limpid. So I gave him money. He thanked me a lot, and his face turned red. He said he would give the money back when he reached his home. I said there was no need to pay the money back and left.

I am afraid that when my classmates know this, they will laugh at me and call me a fool. There are too many swindlers now. They always say they are in trouble, but in fact, they only want to get money. If my parents know about this, they will say I am a little baby who cannot distinguish the fact.

Maybe they are right. But I still believe that man is not a con artist. But from his eyes I can tell he was really in trouble. Why do grown-ups not believe others? Could you tell me if what I did is right? Could you tell me what Americans would do if they met a beggar? I am looking forward to hearing from you.

Sincerely yours, Baby Cao (Hangzhou, Zhejiang)

▲

Dear Baby,

Thank you for sending me such a thoughtful letter. You express your feelings with much sensitivity and sincerity.

You raise a delicate question. There is no easy answer. I often say that these are the three most common words in the English language: It all depends! I wonder if this is also true in Chinese.

The situation you describe is common in America as well as in China and other nations. Poverty is a terrible burden and it is so prevalent. I believe that we must be sympathetic and helpful to all people who are less fortunate than we are. The ability to give is a gift, and I admire your willingness to share this gift with others who are in need.

In this case, you acted with compassion in giving money to a person in need without asking for anything in return. It is true that this man may be a "con artist," and there are many such persons in circulation. Your response was to be generous, and I believe that generosity is a blessing. If you guessed wrong about this particular man, you retained your generosity and he retained his duplicity. Perhaps he will learn a lesson from the kindness you showed him.

I applaud your generosity and your feelings of mercy. There is little danger in doing what you did, and much reward if you were able to help this man. All you could lose is money.

However, there is considerable danger of developing any relationship with a stranger. Perhaps this is what concerned your parents and friends. Unfortunately there are men and women who prowl about looking to entrap young girls and boys. I share this concern and warn you never to go anywhere with a stranger no matter how desperate he (or she) may appear, and no matter what stories he (or she) tells you.

Many young women are being kidnapped either bodily or by false promises. You must never let your generosity extend beyond offering small amounts of money. There is little danger in being swindled, but there is great danger in being led into a relationship which could bring harm or disgrace to you. So, "It all depends" on what you are being asked to do and upon how you judge the person who is asking.

Thank you again for sharing your thoughts with me. Your letter makes me glad to know that there are compassionate young persons like you in this world. Our future depends on you.

With best wishes for happiness and success in your high school and college studies, Bob

Parents and Children

Dear Mr. Herman,

I was too happy to say a word when I read your letter. This is the first time I have received a letter from an American writer. Thank you for your advice and encouragement. It is the best gift I have ever gotten. I think I am the luckiest girl in the world. After I sent my first letter to you, I thought I would not get your letter. Now I know I was wrong. Thanks, Bob and Mahya!

My teacher told me people are good and kind, though her purse had been stolen twice on the bus. If people always blame others, our society will not become better. So I want to be the pioneer. I will remember your advice that it all depends. We want to help others, and we also need to protect ourselves.

Today could I ask another question? As you know, one family in China can only have one child now. In my opinion, some parents love their children too much and pay too much attention to them so that the children cannot do a lot of things they want to do. As children, we do not want to hurt our parents' feelings . . .

Although our parents love us very much, we still want to have our own freedom. I wonder if this happens in the U.S.

I know there are some different ideas between Chinese and Americans. Could you tell me how the parents in the U.S. love their children? Maybe the question is too big; I am just curious about it. I am looking forward to hearing from you again. Thank you!

Sincerely yours, Baby Cao (Hangzhou, Zhejiang)

▲

Dear Baby,

You ask about a very important subject—the relationship between parents and their children. Of course I do not pretend to be an expert on this. I was interested in your description of this relationship in China as you have observed it.

I believe that parents love their children in all cultures although there are many ways that this relationship is expressed. In America there are many cultures. Some tend to be more openly expressive with their feelings than others. In general I feel that parents tend to be over protective, but this is understandable in terms of the dangers that prevail in our modern societies.

My own view is that children want independence, freedom and flexibility. Parents want power and authority. These values may clash over how much freedom children should be permitted to have. Sometimes parents, coming from another generation, do not understand the needs of their children to explore and to make mistakes of their own. And children may not understand the need of parents to be protective and to want to share parental values with their children. All of this may create tensions between the generations, but tensions can be helpful if they lead to greater understanding and tolerance of the opinions of others.

All this has nothing to do with "love". Under all circumstances I assume that there is love between children and their parents. It is the expression of this "love" that we are writing about. It is often hard for parents to "let go," and to observe the changes in their children as they grow and mature. The expression commonly used in America in one of our songs is "Why Can't They Be More Like We Were?" Well, times are changing rapidly, and the present world can be quite different from the "world of our fathers." If you compare the world of your parents' childhood with your present world, I am sure that you will see many differences.

Thank you again for raising such an important topic. It is one that is probably in the minds of many of our readers, whether they are parents or children. In some ways we are all children, and in some ways we all have the desire to be a parent to others.

With warm regards, Bob

▲

Dear Bob,

Thank you for answering my question so patiently and ardently. I was very pleased when I read your second letter.

I think your opinion on parents and children is right. Because of the love between the children and their parents, it often causes some problems. If the contradiction between them is serious, the tragic may happen.

Yesterday when I was watching TV, I saw astonishing news. A boy who was only 16 years old killed his mother! This boy did not study hard, so his mother often blamed him. At last the boy chopped his mother with a kitchen knife . . ..

I still remember three years ago when another boy, who studied very hard in middle school, killed his mother with a hammer. The reason is the same: his mother forced him to study day and night.

The things have caught the attention of the whole society. Why did they kill their mothers, not fathers? Maybe mothers are always chattering about a lot of things with their children. In my opinion, there are some reasons for it. The first reason is that our Chinese students have a lot of pressure because of the population. If we have some unhappy things, we can only share them with friends, not parents.

The second reason is that some young persons do things without thinking. On the other hand, some parents do not really know what their children need, so they do not use the right way to deal with them. And in most Chinese parents' minds, studying is the only way to success. Children who do not study hard will have a hopeless future.

Bob, I really want to know what your opinion is. Could you tell me? I think killing parents is a terrible thing, don't you agree with me?

Best regards, Baby Cao (Hangzhou, Zhejiang)

P.S. I have read your third column. I like the pig and the cow story. The cow said, "Maybe it is because I give while I am still living." I think the meaning of the story will be useful in my future. Thank you for the good story.

▲

Dear Baby,

Thank you for sending me your thoughtful letter and for teaching me about some attitudes toward education in China. It is always a pleasure to know that you are concerned with such important and universal problems.

Your letter raises two separate but related questions (1) the killing of parents, and (2) pressuring children.

Please understand that I am not an expert on either of these matters, but since you ask my judgment, I shall try to oblige.

I can see no justification for any child killing its mother (or for killing its father or grandparents or siblings or anyone else). Killing is a brutal and fatal act. There are no good reasons for settling disagreements by killing. Yes, I agree with you that killing parents is a terrible thing to do.

On your second question, from what you describe, it seems that some parents in China put excessive pressure on their children to study and to perform and to achieve. This is also true in America, and I have seen many unfortunate results of such practice. It is often harmful to both the parents and to their children.

We know that our world is filled with good intentions, but good intentions do not always produce good results. Parents everywhere want the best for their child. Sometimes this can be a matter of wanting prestige or approval for themselves. Some children take this kind of pressure well. They achieve and reach the goals set by their parents. Other children are driven to disappointment, to despair, to, depression and even to death because they cannot perform the way their parents are expecting.

You say that "in most Chinese parents' minds, studying is the only way to success." I am not questioning the motivation of these Chinese parents. I am sure they want the best for their children, as do parents all over this world. However there are other paths to success. Laborers, for example, serve society as well as physicians do. A happy mailman or garbage collector may have a more "successful" life than an unhappy brain surgeon. In fact, one of the most important needs in every society is the need to give dignity to menial work. We do not do this enough in America. I hope you do in China.

I am always in favor of study. There is so much to learn in this world. But study should be enjoyable and not the result of pressure from parents. Certain children have the capability and the motivation to study hard and become highly educated professionals. Other children see their futures in different terms, and one is not necessarily better than the other.

Unfortunately I am not familiar with Chinese society, but I feel certain that if a poll were taken in America, and the American public were asked to decide whether they would rather do without plumbers or without college professors, the vote would be much in favor of eliminating the college professors. All this means is that there are many ways to serve society, and we must give dignity to all persons no matter which occupation or trade they decide to follow.

In some societies, begging is considered the highest level of achievement. In others it may be military service or law or medicine. I feel that there is no perfect ambition and no perfect occupation. We need electricians and carpenters as well as poets and physicians and professors. All are important parts of any successful society. It can be harmful to children if they are pressured to reach goals that are frustrating to them and that they cannot reach without self-damage. This usually results in frictions between parents and children, and these frictions can be harmful to both.

For children to find peace and confidence within themselves may be more important than the level of their work achievement. If we are not able to achieve peace and contentment and confidence within ourselves, we probably will not find it in our professions.

Ms. Cao, you have the ability to unleash long-winded responses from me, and I enjoy giving these to you. I usually tell students that these are the four most important words in the English language: I Could Be Wrong. I would like to know the feelings of our Chinese readers on this important subject.

With best wishes, Bob

Cultures

Dear Bob,

I'm a student in Southwestern China and have learned English for two years.

People often say Americans are good with humor, but when I talk to Americans, I cannot tell. I wonder if humor and jokes are the same. Does humor have to make people laugh as jokes do or anything else?

Please write to me ASAP. Bernie (Bijie, Guizhou)

▲

Dear Bernie,

Thank you for writing to me. I share your interest in humor and have written an entire column on this important subject. Humor means something different to everyone. What is funny to one person may not be funny to another person.

Humor is influenced by culture, by tradition, by personal experiences, and by many more factors.

Humor is a very broad aspect of life. Jokes are one part of humor. Wit is another. Then there is physical humor, the kind that clowns give to us. They make us laugh without telling us any jokes.

I am pleased to know of your interest in humor. It fascinates me. I also like the name "Bernie." It was my father's name.

With warm regards and best wishes for many more laughs, Bob

Education

Hi, Bob,

Nowadays, information changes so quickly. Everyone realizes the importance of continuing their education. If not, they will fall behind in society. So they have to study, even though they don't want to.

Why are adults tired of studying? Under our education system, most of us have to study, teachers force us to, and we have no choice. What's your opinion on this?

Cheng Bo (Shengyang)

▲

Dear Bo,

Thank you for writing to me again. It is true that both technology and current events are moving fast. We can keep up with this rapid pace only by reading, listening, and learning. Technological change is taking place at an alarming rate of speed. We say that if a worker takes a long lunch period, he needs to be retrained.

Learning in today's society is a lifetime process. Those who neglect it will suffer. I hope that you will continue to learn, and to laugh. Learning and laughing make a good pair.

With best wishes, Bob

Knowing Oneself

Hi Bob,

This question has puzzled me for a long time. I still can't solve it. I'm so eager to know myself. I don't know where to start and how to do it. Can you give me some advice?

Yours, Cheng Bo (Shengyang)

▲

Dear Bo,

You ask how to "know oneself." This is one of the most important questions that anyone can ask. It is a basic question that every one of us must ask himself. There is no easy answer to such a universal question. The pursuit of oneself is a lifetime search.

I believe that life consists of windows and mirrors. We have windows to look out of. It is through these windows that we see the world outside us. We also have mirrors that we look into, and it is here that we see the world inside us.

It is easy to look out of our windows and see the wonders of nature, to see our friends and family, and to see the results of years of human labor. It is not so easy to stare into our mirrors and to look for our purpose in life, to look for reasons why we do the things we do and why we think the thoughts that we think.

Our mirrors can give us painful images. It can show us the prejudices that we harbor and the false values that we attach to material things. It can question our desires and our activities. It can produce sadness that we have not achieved our goals. It can make us sorry that we were not more charitable or more loving. It can also give us strength especially if it tells us that we are beautiful and that we are spending much of our time doing and thinking about ways to improve the human condition in our broader society.

Looking into the mirror is what we call "introspection" in English. In spite of its dangers, it should give us a better understanding of who we are. This should be the first step toward asking who we would want to be. A thoughtful person then should have a better basis for deciding what changes are needed to improve and to move on to a more satisfying life.

Of course all of us are constantly changing, and our mirrors should reflect these changes. If we see the same person in the mirror that we saw 20 years ago, it means that there was no change, no growth, and no development.

We do want to be able to understand ourselves. This is the first step toward understanding others. If we know more about our motives, our behavior, our values, and our attitudes, we should be better able to improve our relationships with our families, our friends and colleagues.

Having explored the value of the mirror, we do need to caution ourselves about spending too much time looking inward and not enough time looking outward. Some of my friends spend so much time trying to decide who they are that they are lose their perspective on what is going on outside themselves. I call this "internalizing." A constant probing into ourselves can sap our energies and detract us from important tasks such as the need to be of service to others and the need to improve our society.

You have asked an important question about a delicate subject. If there is an "answer," it is to try to achieve a balance between looking into ourselves and looking out into the broader world that we inhabit. Both viewpoints are necessary for us to survive and prosper in this complicated world.

With warm regards and best wishes, Bob

▲

Hi, Bob,

Thank you for your detailed answer. I will read your e-mail again and again until I can fully understand it. I will take it seriously.

Cheng Bo (Shengyang)

Dear Bob,

Hi, I am Boris, and I am studying at high school in China. When I read your article in *English Salon*, I was very happy.

This year, an American language master is coming here. I want to talk with him very much. But he is the only language master here, and the number of the students in our school is nearly 2,000. It is impossible that every one of us can speak with him. I hope that I can talk to him. Once I talk with him, how shall I talk to him in limited time? Thanks.

Best wishes! Boris (Anda, Heilongjiang)

▲

Dear Boris,

I always enjoy hearing from our readers in China.

If an American language instructor is coming to your school, I hope you will try to speak with him. Please do not be shy about approaching him. I assume that the purpose of his visit is to help the students in your school to learn more English. You can help him by asking him questions which should enable you to learn more English from him.

With warm regards and best wishes, Bob

▲

Bob,

I am so glad to be given such a perfect opportunity to communicate with you on the Internet.

I am wondering if you are keeping your body strong, working very hard, and writing your poems one after another. You are a successful man with rich knowledge and social experience. I hope to make a friend just like you, which must be a gift given by God.

I am an ordinary Chinese student with the dream of speaking gorgeous English so that even native English speakers take me as an American when I am in the U.S. My best hobby is studying English.

Anyway, I want to improve my English in order to communicate with you. Of course, if you want to study Chinese, I won't hesitate to help you! I am not kidding.

Finally, please send my best wishes to your family.

Yours respectfully, Brian Chen (Qingdao, Shandong)

▲

Dear Brian,

Thank you for your wonderful letter. I wish I could express myself in Chinese the way you express yourself in English. You write English very well, and I know that you will be improving even more as you study and practice. It is a privilege to be able to communicate in more than one language. I hope I can continue to share my thoughts with you in my columns.

With warm regards and best wishes for the future, Bob

Anger Management

Dear Bob,

I'm a 24-year-old boy, ambitious and aggressive with a bad temper. I usually quarrel with others and regret it later. I always set high goals for myself and strive to achieve them one by one. I found myself dissatisfied with my job, my position as well as my employers, so I changed jobs frequently: 5 jobs in 3 cities in 2 years. I still feel nervous and unhappy, though others think I've done well enough. The first time I quit, they believed that it was because the company had too many shortcomings, but after 2 or 3 times, they thought that it was my own problem. Maybe I'm too scrutinizing of both others and myself.

I'm not social and have few friends, but all my friends regard me as being very honest, warmhearted, and reliable.

I don't know when I will get a feeling of certainty and fulfillment. So, Bob, would you tell me how you define success and happiness?

Yours, Christian (Shanghai)

▲

Dear Christian,

Thank you for sharing your thoughts and your concerns with me. I wish we could be together so we could discuss them in person. Because this is not possible, here are a few of my reactions to the questions you raise.

You mention having a "bad temper." This could mean several different conditions depending on how severe it is. In this complicated society where we are constantly interacting with each other, it becomes increasingly important to be able to control our emotions. When we lose our tempers with our friends, we are really losing control of emotions and usually showing anger against ourselves. It requires considerable discipline to keep saying to oneself, "I am beautiful and I am smart. I am going to be at peace with myself. I am not going to let anyone else disturb this peace. I believe in myself." Or, just to remind ourselves to "cool it, cool it, it can't be that important."

It is also important to understand that everyone deserves dignity whether we agree with them our not. Because our world has become so competitive, our values and our ambitions often clash with those of our friends. This is why we must constantly remind ourselves that we must be cooperative and compassionate in our dealings with others.

Frequent job changes are not especially bad and not especially good. It depends on the cause. From your letter, it sounds like you may be setting standards of work of your own which may be in conflict with those of your employer. This, of course, leads to tension and dissatisfaction on the part of both you and your employer. In unusual circumstances, your employer will alter its standards because they see the wisdom of yours. More often, it is time to leave a situation where your values are not compatible with those of the company you are with. I assume that this is what you have been doing. There seem to be two alternatives for you. Either you reconsider you own values and standards so that they are more acceptable to others, or you keep moving toward some employment that will enable you to retain the high standards you set for yourself. Maybe you can do both? Please try.

You ask how I would define success. This is complicated. Each of us must define it for ourselves. Unfortunately "success" is most often measured by the amount of wealth one has accumulated, or the position in society one has achieved, or by athletic or academic achievements one has attained. I believe that this is sad. I have seen wealthy men and women lead miserable lives. I have seen great athletics break down completely. I have seen brilliant scholars live in torment. I feel that success must be measured much differently.

For example, I would define success as having achieved peace within oneself, as having the ability to accept change gracefully, and as having an understanding of the brevity of life and the need to be of service to others. Several years ago a famous doctor was giving a lecture on mental health. A man in the audience asked him, "What would you advise a person to do if that person felt a nervous breakdown coming on?" Most people expected him to say, "Consult a psychiatrist." Instead he replied, "Leave your house, go to a poorer part of your town, find someone in need, and do something to help that person." Christian, I think there is a lesson here for all of us.

Your final question asks how I would define happiness. You certainly have the ability to ask the most important questions. I believe that "happiness," like "success," comes from within. The traditional definition of happiness probably would be "having what you want." Maybe we should reverse this and define happiness as "wanting what you have"? I leave it to you to choose which of these definitions you prefer.

Life is not a walk through a field of roses. Life makes many complicated and often irrational demands on all of us. Just as the brook would stop singing if we remove the rocks, even walks through fields of roses can be boring. I believe that you will achieve both success and happiness when you have found ways to use your talents to make this planet a better place to live and work in.

The fact that you are questioning your values and your emotions is a giant first step toward reaching the success and the happiness that you seek. Please never stop questioning. There are no easy answers, and it is the questions that are most important.

With warm regards and best wishes for both success and happiness, Bob

Life's Problems

Dear Bob,

I read your article, "Problems." I agree with your opinions. In our lifelong trip, problems are inevitable. It is these problems that stimulate us and make us progress. However, I think the most important thing is our attitude towards them.

I read the proverbs given in your article. I like them, but I cannot understand one of them, "The brook would stop singing if we removed the rocks." I think that "the rocks" reflect the snags in life. If this is true, what does the sentence mean? Why does the brook stop singing after the rocks have been removed?

Would you please give me your opinion on it? Thank you.

Yours, Christin (Ningbo, Zhejiang)

▲

Dear Christin,

You interpreted my comments on "Problems" correctly. I was merely trying to explain that a life without problems would be a dull and uneventful life. As long as there is life and as long as there are people inhabiting this life there will be problems. The problems are there. What is important is how we deal with them.

"The brook would stop singing if we removed the rocks" is meant to be a metaphor for life, and it relates to the question of "problems." Most of us enjoy the sound of a bounding brook. The sound that we enjoy comes from the water splashing against the rocks. A brook that runs without any impediment would be a silent brook. This would be less appealing to our ears.

In life, too, without problems there would be no joy and no sorrow. It would also be "soundless." This would be hard to imagine because we are forced to deal with problems from the time we are born, and probably even before then while we are developing in the womb.

With best wishes, and I hope you have problems that are easy and pleasant to deal with, Bob

▲

Dear Bob,

I was very glad to receive your letter. I really appreciate you for solving my problem.

I wrote to you without any hope of your response. How surprised I was when I saw your name in my mailbox!

From now on, I will have no hesitation to write to you whenever I have problems.

Best wishes, Christin (Ningbo, Zhejiang)

Tradition

Hello! Bob!

I am not sure if you still remember me, a reader of *Overseas English* and a member of the Foreign Language Faculty of Ningbo University. I really like reading your articles.

I am writing to ask for your help. I am doing research on the "Chinese Traditional Culture." I would like to get some thoughts from foreigners. I hope you can tell me what you think about it. Thank you!

I hope it won't bother you.

Best Wishes! Yours, Christin (Ningbo, Zhejiang)

▲

Dear Christin,

I do remember you and our past correspondence. I feel privileged to be writing to a member of the Foreign Language Faculty of Ningbo University.

In response to your question about Chinese Traditional Culture, I wish I was better informed on all aspects of it. I try to spend as much of my time as possible reading and trying to understand this rich culture and history. Of course I have the limitation of not being able to read in Chinese. This is a formidable handicap. I apologize for not being a scholar on this important subject.

Since I was a child, and that was many, many years ago, I have been fascinated by the origin and development of Chinese thought and by the history of Chinese civilization. I believe that western countries can learn much from this study. It is unfortunate that most of the study of history in the western countries has been devoted to its development from the Hebrew, Greek and Roman cultures. Of course we owe most of our tradition, our thought, our art and architecture, our language, and our literature to western traditions.

In spite of the general neglect of Chinese studies in America, I am thrilled to study and reflect over as many aspects of Chinese traditional culture as I can. Of course it is not possible for me to summarize what I have learned by means of this brief letter. But, here are a few of the topics that I have found most enlightening:

The Analects of Confucius continue to fascinate me. So many of the writings from the Han dynasty are treasures that should be read and reread. I have also learned much from reading Mencius and Xunzi, with their emphasis on the preservation of tradition and moral cultivation. Their discussions of government and human nature are very relevant to today's problems. The Daoist teachings continue to fascinate me, especially the passages from the Laozi.

The Book of Songs from the early Zhou period has taught me much about love and marriage and work and war. Wang Fu's essay on Friendship and Getting Ahead is as important today as when it was written two thousand years ago. Have you read "A Woman's Hundred Years" which was recorded in the Great Tang dynasty around 900? This is a delicious poem, which I heartily recommend.

I believe that no one can be truly "educated" today who is not familiar with the "Three Teachings" (Daoism, Buddhism, and Confucianism). These are full of learning and understanding and insights into what is important about life and death.

Best wishes for your studies, and warm regards, Bob

War and Peace

Mr. Herman,

I was deeply moved by your column in the November issue of Overseas English, "The Universe." It is a very beautiful article for its ideas as well as its words.

The world that you describe in your article has no armaments, no wars, no cares, no hierarchies. The people are full of mercy, sincerity, respect for others, compassion, kindness, and amicability to our lovely nature. But the real world is reality, where we have to struggle for our next meal, where we have to follow whatever path our parents select for us, where we have to violate our ethics by following "game rules" in society. People in China always say that as one grows, he will gain intelligence, experience, and knowledge, but he will, at the same time, lose truth, honesty, innocence, and he will believe that it is the necessary cost of growth.

I am a college student of 21, and I don't think so. I worry this price will give us a world without moorings, without honesty, without human connections, and will turn everyone into a soul on the verge of a self-centered psychotic breakdown.

Of course we need bread and water, but we also need fresh air, clear skies, and mutual concern for each other. I don't know what how Americans balance the two aspects, living in the most developed country, both economically and culturally. I also want to know your ideas on this topic. I look forward to hearing from you very much!

Yours sincerely, Christina (Chengdu, Sichuan)

▲

Dear Christina,

Your letter is an inspiration to me. Thank you for expressing your thoughts so elegantly. Yes, my universe is an ideal place with kindness replacing war, and with an abundance of good feeling replacing hate and competition.

As you write, this is far from the reality of our present Universe. And, as you say, it is the real world with all the demands it makes on us. We need food and shelter and the means to acquire these necessities. But, does this mean that we need to sacrifice our values or our ideals? I think not! We must try to distinguish "necessities" from "luxuries." I believe that in our present Universe many have lost their ideals in the pursuit of luxuries that have become obscene alongside of the poverty that exists.

As we grow in knowledge and experience we do not have to lose our honesty or our mercy or our feelings for others who are less fortunate than us. If we let our knowledge become wisdom, we will understand the importance of human connections and we will be aware of our mortality. Because our individual existence on this earth is so brief, there should be no time for hate or acquisitiveness.

You ask about countries with highly developed economic progress. We must be careful not to confuse economic progress with an improvement in the human condition. Very often they are not the same. Economic progress does provide good plumbing, temperature controls, better means of communication, and lots more "goodies." But our measure of economic progress does not always tell the whole story.

Economic progress is usually measured by what is called the "national product." This measure of economic success includes spending for advertising of cigarettes and other socially undesirably items. It also includes spending for television programs which glorify violence, and spending for a huge surplus of goods which accumulate in homes and warehouses, and it includes mountains of weapons of destruction.

This economic measure does not consider the beauty of our poetry or the quality of our air, or the quality of our education, or the wisdom of our learning, or our compassion or our wit or our courage or our kindness toward each other. It measures mostly "stuff" which tends to clutter our lives.

I am glad that, as a 21-year-old student, you are worried over this situation. I like your description of a "world without moorings, without honesty, without human connections." This is a world that you and I have not made. However, it is the world we are living in, and as long as there are young persons like you who are concerned over its present plight, I feel that there is hope for the future being better.

Again, thank you for your thoughts, and keep hold of your ideals. They are a treasure that no one can take away from you.

Respectfully yours, Bob

▲

Dear Mahya,

Bob's letter is the most affecting article I have read, graceful and thoughtful, full of philosophy and insight. When I read the e-mail from Bob, it seems that Bob is talking to me, with wisdom twinkling in his eyes. Yes, I can feel that and I can imagine that scene, although there is such a long distance between China and America.

Thank you very much for giving me a chance to converse with such an excellent writer like Bob.

I like your column very much and hope it becomes more and more popular, and that Bob can write more and more excellent work for us.

Yours sincerely, Christina (Chengdu, Sichuan)

Poetry

Dear Mr. Herman,

From reading your column, "Adventures of the Mind," in *Overseas English*, I know you are a famous poet. I am wondering whether you would tell me what my poem is like and what we can call a poem. I just wrote down what I saw and what I thought.

A Bird Is Singing

In a green tree, a black bird is singing
Sounding like a troll joyfully ringing
Such a sound without any resistance
It is the sound of full independence

He was born, he grew up he's flying
He sleeps, and he is living
He is doomed to pass away some day
He knows that's the definite fate, I dare say

But he is lively and he is happy
Perhaps he never thinks he is lucky or unlucky
Maybe life is just like this
Live a natural life just as it is

Unknown World

The day is falling with a light red
All the birds are returning home fed
Wandering on a hill, lonely and fled
What about my traveling to the other unknown side
In which cavern can it place me
What splendor view can I see
Compared with the present world
what difference there may be
Some day I am to be waited there surely
I dare say it's my definite destiny
Should I be sad or happy

No Title

Lose all, seeming to get all
Forget all, seeming to have all
Love all, seeming to ruining all
You are none, seeming you are all

That's the highest state of enjoyment
By it the deepest experience I meant
Without the shortest moment
What's difference between you and the environment

Please don't laugh at me. I want to increase my ability to appreciate English literature including the poem "Nothings" written by you. Would you give me your opinion on them?

With best wishes for happiness and success in your career,
Wang Chuffing

▲

Dear Chuffing,

Thank you for sending me your beautiful poetry. I admire what you wrote, and I believe that you have a fine future as a poet. You express your feelings very well and show much sensitivity and originality.

"A Bird Is Singing" is a tender poem. You make your black bird live and die so gracefully. Your choice of words is splendid. "Doomed to pass away someday" is a good line. This is a fine story of nature and you give it poetic form.

"Unknown World" is another fine poem. It deals with death in a very sensitive manner. Death is one of the great themes in all literature including poetry, and you confront it with dignity and mystery. When Socrates was dying, his last words were purported to be: "The hour of departure has arrived. Me to die and you to live. Which is better, only god knows." You ask "Should I be sad or happy?" This is a profound question, and you state it with grace and brevity. Very good!

"No Title" has strong feelings and good rhythm. I like the first stanza very much. Your second stanza is not as clear as it could be. I think you are struggling too much for rhyming. The last line needs changing. It is not clear enough.

I hope you will continue to write poetry. It must be hard for you to write so well in English. I hope you are also writing in Chinese. This should be easier for you.

Please keep writing and keep imagining. Imagination is one of the basic ingredients of poetry, and you have much of it to use.

With best wishes and warm regards, Bob

Language

Hi, Bob,

I am a college student at Nanjing University of Technology.

My hobby is listening to English music. Now I am having trouble with the song, "I Knew I Loved You," sung by Savage Garden. Would you mind explaining it to me? God bless you!

Yours, Cinderella (Nanjing, Jiangsu)

Dear Cinderella,

I was not familiar with the song you mentioned, but Mahya sent me a copy. It is a beautiful love song. It is very romantic and quite mystical. It expresses total love and a feeling that love was destined to be, that it was part of the design of the Universe that we (the two lovers) were to meet and to love.

As you know, "love" can be quite complicated. I think it is one of the greatest unsolved mysteries in modern life. Because "love" is so universal and so confusing, I attempted to write some of my thoughts about it. I believe that these will be published in the February issue of *Overseas English*.

With warm regards, Bob

▲

Hi, Bob,

I am delighted to hear from you.

What is the meaning of, "To make each day count"? I would appreciate it if you could help me.

Yours, Cinderella (Nanjing, Jiangsu)

▲

Dear Cinderella,

This is a good question. The phrase means that we have only so many days alive on this earth, and we should try to make every one of these days have some meaning. By making them "count" does not mean numbering them. English can be a very confusing language, and this is an example of how it can be misleading.

I am glad that you asked this question. Thank you for reading my column and for thinking about what it contains. I hope that you will make your days "count." We have little control over the number of days that we have, but we do have much control over how we use them. Let's all try to use our days productively and in the service of our fellow human beings.

With warm regards, Bob

▲

Hi, Bob,

I am so happy to read your letter and to learn a lot from you.

I have some difficulty with remembering all the meanings of a phrase. Take "go up," for example. I know it means "to be raised," "to become higher," and so on. However, it also means "to be destroyed by fire or an explosion," but I can't understand how the proposition "up" is related to an explosion. Could you explain this?

Thank you very much. Cinderella (Nanjing, Jiangshu)

▲

Dear Cinderella,

I am happy that you are continuing with your English studies. I admire anyone who tries to make sense out of this crazy language that we call English. If I were not born into it, I fear that I could never learn to speak or write it.

You ask about our word "up," and about some of the ways we use it. It does mean becoming higher like in "going up the mountain" or "rising up" the social ladder. We also use "up" in the sense of being eliminated or destroyed as in "the building was blown up." We also equate it with "finished" when we say "his time was up," and in an entirely different sense to mean "equality" when we say the score is "seven-up" which means that the score is tied.

To prove how strange and unpredictable the English language is, the word "up" can even have no meaning. For example, "Hurry up" and "Hurry" have exactly the same meaning. The "up" adds nothing to the "Hurry."

I wish I could say that there are rules for using "up," but there are none. My only advice is to accept the fact that the English language is complex and irrational. It can only be learned by practicing it.

Best wishes for success in your studies, Bob

▲

Dear Bob,

I am a loyal reader of *English Salon*. I have read this great magazine for almost 5 years. I met you recently and am eager to communicate with you.

I like English very much and have spent a lot of time on it, but recently I am finding that learning English seems to become increasingly difficult. My efforts appear to produce less obvious results. I often hesitate when confronted with the vast untouched areas of English vocabulary and usage which fall outside of the scope of basic textbooks. I feel uneasy because the language I thought I knew now appears to consist of a bewildering variety of idioms, clichés, and phrases with different meaning in different contexts. The more I learn, the less I know.

I have passed the CET-4, which qualifies me for the undergraduate degree. Some of my classmates are slack in their studies of English. It seems they learn it only for passing exams. I cannot agree with them.

English is becoming more popular in China. Mastering it is a necessary job, so I really need your guidance to help me make progress towards fluency.

Thank you very much for enduring my poor English. Thanks to Mahya Zhang. You must be a successful English learner. I also expect your advice.

Hope you both have a nice day!

Yours, Destiny (Shijiazhuang, Hebei)

Dear Destiny,

Your English is excellent. I admire the skill with which you put your sentences together and your skill in selecting the proper words. You are so far advanced that all I can suggest is that you find persons to practice with, and that you continue to study publications like *English Salon*.

English is a difficult language. Many of our idioms are idiotic. They make no sense unless you know the situation that they are derived from. Our slang is provincial even in America and much of it changes rapidly from one decade to the next. American movies and television are good sources for learning current English usage even though much of it is poor English.

Mahya Zhang has become bilingual even though she has been living in America for only a few years. This is partly because she is eager to learn and because she has so many opportunities to practice. You have such an excellent beginning. From now on all you need is exposure to English and practice with friends. You must also try to lose any inhibition you might have. I know you are on the verge of fluency. Keep at it.

With best wishes, Bob

▲

Dear Bob,

Thank you for your advice. I was so excited to read your letter. I will keep at it, I promise. You have given me confidence. Thank you!

First, you said to "find persons to practice with." Do you mean to just practice oral English or to do something else?

Second, when I write something, especially when I write to you, I need to think about choosing better words and phrases. I even resort to a dictionary. This takes a long time. Do you think it is a process one must experience?

Yours, Destiny (Shijiazhuang, Hebei)

Dear Destiny,

There is not much I can add to my last letter to you. Keep trying to practice speaking and listening to English as much as you can. Of course it is not easy to write in English. Many Americans also find it difficult to write in good English. Using a dictionary is a good way to learn. It will help you to choose exactly the right word for what you wish to say.

With best wishes, Bob

▲

Dear Mr. Herman,

I learned about you from *Overseas English*. You have solved problems for many people, and I think your advice is very reasonable, even though some of our questions only exist in china.

I'm a second year college student. I have never talked with a foreigner, and I'm afraid to. I don't know why. I am very afraid to attend an oral English class. I think I can write very well, but I can't speak well, so I am asking you for help. Can you give me suggestions? Thank you!

Yours sincerely, Evelyn

▲

Dear Evelyn,

If you will try to study and practice speaking English, I know that you will become excellent at it. I wish I could help you by speaking with you, but this is not possible. The best advice is to practice speaking and to not be afraid of making mistakes. Listening can also be of help. Sometimes this can be done by listening to English spoken over the radio or on television.

If you can write as well as you do, speaking should come easily. Be brave, talk in English no matter how it sounds. It will improve as you practice.

With warm regards and respectfully yours, Bob

Dear Bob,

Thank you for your letter, I think your words are very reasonable. I'm a very shy girl. My classmates always encourage me, but it's useless, so I decided to attend an oral class. Do you think it is necessary?

Yours sincerely, Evelyn

▲

Dear Evelyn,

I am pleased that you are taking oral English courses. I am sure that your spoken English will improve, but this will only happen if you practice speaking. Please do not be afraid of making mistakes. Most of the people here in America make big mistakes in speaking their English, and they have been speaking since childhood.

You write English very well, and it should not be long before you are able to speak fluently.

With warm regards and best wishes, Bob

▲

Dear Bob,

Thank you so much for your response and your time.

I do agree that every one of us has problems in life. My troubles are not necessarily bigger than that of others. Disasters happen every day, so why should I be exempt?

Life is so short, and it is really foolish to waste time worrying about things that may never happen. It is useless to worry too much even if bad things do happen. Only by struggling through troubles will a man grow up.

Recently, I've read a passage that includes the sentence, "Love as if you've never been hurt!" It makes me feel better and encourages me a lot.

Yours truly, Evy

Self-Confidence

Dear Herman,

I read your column in *Overseas English*, and now I have something to consult you about. I am very glad to have this opportunity to write to you.

I am 21 years old, but I am just 142 cm tall. It is a sad thing for me. Furthermore, my teeth are bad, and they are not white at all. I am not a beautiful girl. I know that clearly, and I regret that badly.

These drawbacks of my appearance have influenced my life. I have never had a boyfriend. I always lack confidence in public. I believe nobody will like me. They consider me an ugly girl at first sight. Maybe my image will bore them. Perhaps this will affect my career in the future. Oh, I am so unhappy.

Yours, Cindy (Shenyang, Jiaoning)

▲

Dear Cindy,

I feel sorry that you feel a lack of confidence in yourself because of your appearance. But, at the same time, I am glad that you are reaching out for advice. This is a good sign because it shows that you have a bright spark of life that is waiting to be nurtured.

It is this spark of life, this energy that you have, which is more important than mere appearance. Most activities and accomplishments in life do not depend on how tall we are or how white our teeth are. If you could throw your energy past worrying about your teeth or your height, it will lead you to gain confidence and to a successful career.

We need to understand that our imperfections are what make us beautiful. This is even true with nature. Fish cannot live in pure water. They feed on imperfections.

Beauty can come from within. If we can train ourselves to believe that we are beautiful, it is a big step toward appearing beautiful to others. Real beauty comes from the energy we give and not from how tall we are. I once described an attractive young woman I knew as "a beautiful lamp that was not lighted." Better to be an ordinary lamp that is aglow with light.

When I walked past our local pond as a child, I noticed the baby swans, and thought how ugly, ungainly and awkward they were. It was a shock and pleasant surprise when I saw the same ones as adult swans, beautiful, stately, and graceful. This is similar to the story of The Ugly Duckling written by Hans Christian Anderson. I urge you to read it.

So, Cindy, I ask you to try to focus your energies and thoughts outward, toward the goals you wish to accomplish, toward things you can laugh at, toward persons you like to be with, toward all that nature has to offer to you. This will be in place of focusing your energies inward where they are wasted because they lead only to worrying about your physical appearance.

Twenty-one is a delightful age. Please try to enjoy it and learn to look forward to the many more years ahead. I believe that your search for confidence will be rewarded.

With warmest regards, Bob

▲

Dear Dr. Herman,

Thank you for writing back so quickly.

I know what is more important in my life because of your words. Now I have more assurance to strive for my future. The little black swan was doomed to become a white swan, but I must make efforts to be a beautiful swan. However, I am willing to try and to accept the results.

Thank you very much! Cindy (Shenyang, Jiaoning)

▲

Dear Mahya,

I have just read the passage in Bob's column. I've read it several times. That's because so many ideas flood my mind in a short time that I need to get better understanding of them.

I have just graduated from a college, yet the passage makes me ponder over so much of my experience on the college campus. I find myself not being able to remain in peace.

Bob's writing has begun to influence me. "You will learn to distinguish between the authority of ideas and the idea of authority."

After reading Bob's words, I felt a sense of relief. What Bob says is not as complicated as I had thought. I do appreciate many of his ideas.

I like Bob's column so much. It is like a true friend to exchange ideas with or a window through which I can get a new view of life. Thank you so much for all you have done for us.

Yours sincerely, Claudia (Shanghai, Liaoning)

▲

Dear Claudia,

Mahya shared your letter with me. Your letter shows that you are a profound and thoughtful person.

Please do not allow your college experience to be negative. Your ability to digest and to analyze complex ideas shows that you are already an educated person, and that your thirst for more knowledge and understanding has not been diminished.

Being at peace with yourself is vital. There are many paths to inner peace. Your alive mind and search for truths will lead you along one of these paths.

I admire your ability to express your feelings and to reach for new meanings. Life is filled with ambiguities and contradictions. It is not like a cookie jar which we try to fill with half baked "truths." Please keep learning and questioning. The future belongs to you. I feel that a serious thinker like you is going to have a full and satisfying life.

With best wishes, Bob

Happiness

Dear Bob,

I have read your article, "The Universe," in *Overseas English*, and then I got to read your letter in *English Salon*. Your poems always gave me a deep impression and made me think more. I cannot help writing this letter to you.

Others may think that everything in my life goes well. As a senior in high school, I only have to study. (In fact I wonder if I have the ability to do anything else.) In 150 days, I will become a college student.

I don't think you understand education in China, but I am sure that you can imagine the pressure if there are more than 5.7 million students competing against you. As an outstanding student, getting into the best university is no longer my own business, but my responsibility, so I cannot relax, or all previous work will be undone. . . .

But life is really boring in my eyes. The worst thing is my loss of enthusiasm. Sometimes I act so calm and so sensible. More and more, I find that a confident girl can be so weak. I even cry for no reason. I am easily moved. That is a strange feeling.

At the age of 18, I should say youth is bitter, though I do know that it is the most voluble time in one's life. I also believe that everyone has had such growing pains for no reason or for many reasons.

In fact, I don't need to support my family. My parents love me so much and take good care of me. I should be satisfied with my life. When I realize the nice things I own, I should be happy. Why not?

Happiness is an attitude and a choice. I always imagine my future life and dream, but I do not enjoy the present. I don't know how to fall in love with the life I am living. What I am chasing for on earth? Life is just ambiguous victories and vague defeats.

Then the strange feeling appears all the time: What is the essence of that strange and bitter miracle of life which I feel so poignantly, so unutterably, with such a bitter pain and joy? I am rich and also poor; I am mighty, but I have nothing.

Well, so much for that. I hope you write back soon. Take Care!

Sincerely yours, Connie (Tianjin)

▲

Dear Connie,

Thank you so much for sharing your feelings with me. I learned much from your letter. For a young woman of 18 years you have so much wisdom about life. Yes, life is not an easy path to walk through. It is filled with uncertainty and doubts, and it is temporary. You write this very well. The following phrase is said to be one of the most important in the English language: "And this, too, shall pass away."

Life certainly is brief. This may be discouraging because it means that everything that we possess will become nothing. But it may also be challenging because it means that we must concentrate all our efforts over a short period of time. It also means that we must live every minute of every day because every day that is lost is never regained.

You are so correct when you write that "Happiness is an attitude and a choice." Of course circumstances do govern much of what we do. Some of us are more privileged than others. From your letter, I assume that you are very privileged. The love from your parents and the care that they give to you give you the greatest of privilege. How you use your privilege is your choice as you tell me it is.

Connie, above all, we must consider life as a "gift," and yours seems to be a very special gift. You ask what you are chasing for on earth. I believe that we are chasing after love and friendship and the feeling that we have some purpose in being on this planet. The supreme purpose might be to make this planet more livable for other persons especially for persons who have not been given the gifts that we have.

Connie, I do not give advice. To give advice makes it seem like one comes from a superior position. As a human being, I share with you all of the challenges and the frustrations of modern living. When I feel as you do, my personal experience has been to look outside myself. Instead of dwelling on my internal doubts and even my lack of enthusiasm, my personal experience has been to look out to others who may be less fortunate and to try to help them. To be introspective can be enriching. But to spend too much of our time in what we call "soul searching" can be harmful and not very rewarding.

You write so beautifully and you have a sensitive nature. These are virtues that you should take advantage of. Please continue to learn and to feel and to think. And add to these some laughter and some enjoyment. Life is a serious matter. But it can also be funny especially because there are so many funny people in it—people like me, and perhaps you. So let's try to be funny every so often so we can laugh at ourselves. Let's assume that life is a big joke, that nothing makes any sense in the long run, but it is the only life we have. It is a big challenge and we are going to make the most of it. We are going to learn from it. We are also going to laugh at it. But we are going to enjoy it.

With warmest regards and best wishes, Bob

Dear Bob,

Thank you for your letter. I was excited to receive it and read it carefully many times. It's amazing that a foreigner who lives under different circumstances can understand me so well, and I'm also glad to see that even I can express myself clearly in English. I feel quite well now.

I have just described my feelings, but I haven't told you about what happened in my life that has made me sad. However, it's true that when I look back, it seems to me that I have learned a lot. Frustration makes success more fulfilling, and loss makes the next achievement more meaningful.

I am glad that I've shared my feelings with you. The mind is just like a parachute; it is only useful when it is open. You're kind to read my words. You have taught me a lot.

You are a good listener and also a patient teacher, but I still like to consider you as a friend who is sincere.

Take care and best wishes! Connie (Tianjin)

Parables

Dear Bob,

I'm a student. Your column has enriched my knowledge. Some of this can't be learned from textbooks.

At the end of the story called "The Businessman & Fisherman," you wrote, "There may be a lesson here for all of us." I don't know what the lesson is. Also, I want to know whose attitude is right, the businessman's or the fisherman's. If you can tell me, I'll be very grateful.

Yours faithfully, Peggy (Qingdao, Shandong)

▲

Dear Peggy,

The story about the fisherman and the businessman can be confusing. I was trying to explain that sometimes we do not think enough about our ambitions. We hope for all kinds of luxuries and then do not know what to do with them. We accumulate possessions and fame, and then we become captive to these same possessions and fame.

We are often dissatisfied with our simple pleasures and strive for a more fancy life. The fisherman was content to fish and love, and he led a simple life. After he was enticed into changing for a more elaborate and richer life, he began to yearn for an easier life of fishing and loving. There is a moral to this story: Be careful what you wish for, because there is a good chance that you will get your wish.

Sometimes we envy persons who have fame or riches, but we do not know the effects of leading a complicated existence or the personal price paid for having achieved this fame or wealth. This is not an easy topic to explain because we do not want to eliminate ambition from our lives. I will be writing more on this subject in future articles. Please keep reading and questioning.

With warm regards, Bob

▲

Dear Bob,

I'm a freshman in China and a faithful reader of your column. However, this time I do not like the story very much.

What the businessman said is completely different from what the fisherman did. To the fisherman, his life is just like a circle. It is meaningless. The businessman is the opposite. He went outside the circle, experiencing challenge and competition. All of this adventure makes up our wealth. Then the businessman came back, full of wisdom. Aren't they the same? The fisherman would never own what the successful businessman had.

This is my first letter in English, and I will work harder like the businessmen to achieve success.

Best wishes, Crystal (Hefei, Anhui)

▲

Dear Crystal,

You express yourself very well, and I value your insights. Your analysis of the fisherman story is very interesting, and I appreciate your comments.

It is true, as you said, that the fisherman who has completed the business cycle is not the same as the fisherman was at the beginning. He does have more experience and perhaps more wisdom to draw upon. The point of the story is to show that the lifestyle we aim for may be closer than we think. Ambition may lead us back to where we began.

I applaud your desire to "work harder like the business-man to achieve success." Go to it. We need more persons like you to invigorate our society, to pump energy into life, and not to be satisfied with a dull lazy existence. But, please also keep in mind what you will do with your success as a businessperson. Will you use it for the benefit of your fellow human beings, or will you use it to acquire more stuff for yourself and live a selfish satisfied life of luxury?

If you use your success in business to make life better for others, this seems more socially useful than retiring to a fisherman's village. I believe that our greatest goal must be to combine our individual harmony with a broader social harmony. I think you will be doing this during your life.

With best wishes for success, Bob

▲

Dear Sir,

I like your column very much. However, I cannot agree totally on the last story you gave us, the donkey story.

If the difficulties are big enough, we can live to step up over the stones, but if there are just minor troubles, sometimes we cannot even tell what the problems are. Only when there are too many, we suddenly discover their presence, but it's too late! When all the troubles are minor, how can we step over them?

Perhaps I am a little pessimistic, but life is always realistic, isn't it?

Respectfully yours, Evy

▲

Dear Evy,

I enjoyed reading your comments on my donkey story. Yes, it is true that we can often learn to cope with our biggest problems. This is probably because they are so great and so urgent that we put all of our energies to them.

I agree with you that it is the small problems in life that can bother us the most. In the jungle, for example, it is the gnats that trouble us the most, not the elephants! But life would be dull without problems. Every day would end at eight o'clock in the morning if there were no problems.

How we deal with our problems is a good measure of how we are enjoying this brief journey through life that all of us are experiencing. It has been said that pessimism is a mark of superior intellect. This seems to be true for you. My advice is to deal with your pessimism in a constructive way and learn to enjoy coping with your problems, whether they are big or small.

Best wishes, Bob

▲

Dear Bob,

Do you remember me?

You can't imagine how important your positive remarks and praise are to me. I appreciate you very much. Maybe you don't know that you, using your wisdom and easily-understood stories, have changed families for the better and have changed many youngsters' attitudes to their lives. You set a good example for our youth.

Now I am starting at the beginning of the circle. I have a long way to go, but I will never forget my faith, dedicating myself to human beings and to the world.

With best wishes, Crystal (Hefei, Anhui)

▲

Dear Crystal,

I can feel the sincerity and the deep feelings that you express. I am especially pleased that my thoughts have some meaning to you and to your life. With so much strife and bitterness in this world, it is so important that each of us try to bring kindness and compassion to those people that we can relate to.

I admire you for all you are doing and thinking. Please never give up. The future belongs to persons like you who are trying to improve life for all human beings.

With warm regards, and best wishes, Bob

Who Are "Americans"?

Bob and Mahya,

I am excited that there is a channel through which I can converse with you. After reading the letter Bob wrote in *English Salon*, I believe he is a man who is full of knowledge. Bob, I agree with your opinions, especially your belief that the fact that we are not familiar with each other will be our big advantage.

Who are Americans? How do they live? Only several years ago, many Chinese might say that Americans drive their cars at high speeds, can have sex after only having a look, and can do anything they want without thinking of others. At the same time Americans might think Chinese people are poor. I think there is much prejudice between us.

Many Americans travel to China. Many Chinese people see news about America from the TV and computer. We have gotten to know each other more and more. Though we are still not familiar with each other, we can become familiar in time. We will learn many things from each other. We have different ways of thinking, different roads to travel, and different cultures to develop. Because of our differences, we attract each other. This will be our big advantage.

Hope to hear from you.

Best wish to you, Flowermouse

Dear Flowermouse,

Thank you for your comments on how Americans and Chinese view each other. This is such an important subject and it has such vital worldwide implications. We are all living on a planet which is increasingly vulnerable to being blown into bits. Modern technology has given many nations the capability of destroying other nations, and it has also given nations time for retaliatory strikes. This technology consists of such evil weapons as biological agents, chemical agents, and nuclear weapons. One of the irrefutable facts of our time is that every day nuclear weapons are becoming easier and cheaper to make.

This is a grim picture but it is a realistic one. It means that every nation has the responsibility of insuring that these weapons of great destruction are never used. Because every nation has the capability to make war, war must be made obsolete. The best way of accomplishing this is to remove frictions that may be developing between nations. This requires greater understanding and greater acceptance of differences among people and nations in all parts of the planet.

The responsibility for peaceful and compassionate relationships belongs everywhere. No person and no nation can wiggle out of the need for peace and friendship. The survival of this planet depends upon mutual understanding and support among all nations. We must eliminate war, or war will eliminate us!

Your letter asks specifically about Chinese-American relationships, but I wanted to let you know my feelings on a global scale. Because China and America are the most powerful nations, I believe they have a special responsibility for promoting better understanding and for leading the way toward peaceful solutions to the world's problems.

You ask how Chinese and American people view each other. This is an important question. Because I know so little about China I am not able to judge how Chinese view Americans. I am sure that the view differs according to individual experiences that persons might have. Television and

the computer are having strong influences over our percep-
tions of each other. The computer enables us to communicate
much more easily with each other. I hope that your Chinese
friends will not judge America by what you see on American
television. Unfortunately some of our television programs
present a distorted view of American life. This is sad, and I
apologize for it. Of course some television programs do show
various aspects of American life, and there is much that can
be learned about America from watching these programs.
The sex and violence that you see on America television are
primarily aimed at making money for their advertisers and are
not an indication of our daily behavior.

It is not easy to describe America to foreigners. America
is a vast conglomerate of people and cultures. Our population consists almost entirely of persons who have left their
homelands and migrated to America. These immigrants came
from all parts of the world - from Asia, from Africa, from
Latin America, from Europe, and from Australia. Each immi-
grant brought a different culture and a different set of values.
America has been called a huge "melting pot." This description can be misleading because it implies that this swirling
influx of immigrants has been reduced to a common denomi-
nator, that it has produced "an American." Instead we find
that America is more of a mosaic where many cultures and
many nationalities retain their distinct personalities while
living together within a single nation. There are enclaves of
Chinese, and Italians, and Greeks, and Latin Americans, and
other peoples living in America in their own neighborhoods.
Many of these retain their own cultural values while they
adapt to present day changes. It is not easy to describe an
average American or a typical American viewpoint.

I am also not an expert on how Americans view China.
There are many different views depending on the circumstances of the viewer. I believe that the vast majority of
Americans, like the vast majority of Chinese, want peace and
friendship between our two nations. Both China and America
have suffered through generations of war and violence in our
histories. Because of the dangers of conflict, and the horrors

of mass destruction, all of our peoples must be determined to reach deeper understanding of our different cultures and of each other. This is imperative. The only alternative is global combustion. And I believe that it is the special responsibility of all Chinese and all Americans to impress this need for mutual understanding on our neighbors in other countries.

So, my friend, this is my response to your important inquiries. Please know that I write to you as a private person living in America. I do not represent any governmental agency, and I do not pretend to speak for America in general. These are my personal views. I do feel strongly that people everywhere have more in common than they have differences. We all share the same basic needs for existence and we all depend upon the same need for the survival of this beautiful planet earth. Maybe we can encourage better communication and better understanding through my column. I hope so.

With warm regards and best wishes, Bob

Life

Dear Bob,

Thanks for your reply. I was so excited. Your ideas inspire me. I learned much from your letter. I've read it several times, and each time I can discover some new knowledge to absorb. I still want to share something with you concerning your letter.

Through your lines I understand the meaning of life and death more deeply. Although they seem to be mysterious, when we look into them, they are ordinary tasks that we have to confront.

A few days ago I paid a visit to my father's friend who has cancer. Facing death, he never complained about his bad fortune, nor did he seem a little bit scared. Moreover, smiles were always seen on his face. I know he has chosen the right attitude.

Visiting my father's friend and reading your letter has led me to conclude that we must cherish the time God has given us.

This leads to my second thought. I still remember in your last letter you said, "If we choose to live, then we must try to live to the fullest. This means to give the highest purpose to our lives." I am a lucky girl. I've entered my ideal university, and I am studying my favorite subject, English. Still, I am confused and lost.

Compared to you, Bob, I'm just nobody. I don't have any great purpose like you. What I am concerned about is only my future. But sometimes I wonder, if my future can't be promised, how can I devote myself to others and the world?

I need your help.

With my best wishes!

Yours, Gladys Lee (Guangzhou, Guangdong)

▲

Dear Gladys,

It was a pleasure to receive your letter and to know that we are concerned with similar feelings. I do consider life a special gift even though it is so brief. Each of us has a finite number of years. We are hostages to Time.

You mention being "lost" and being without a purpose. Gladys, you are too young to be lost. I think you let yourself become too easily discouraged. Your purpose is clear to me. It is to live, and to live productively for yourself and for others. There is never enough time for being discouraged. Your father's friend should serve as a good example for you. Even though he had little to look forward to, he did not complain about his bad fortune. You mentioned the smile on this man's face. Remember, Gladys, that a smile is the easiest and cheapest way to improve your looks!

You have achieved so much and in such little time. To be able to study at your ideal university is a blessing. It is an achievement that you should be proud of and should make it a base for future achievements. There must be millions of young Chinese who would envy you and your position. It is always good to be able to expand and clarify your purpose in life. I do this constantly, but I am careful not to let myself become discouraged just because I am unable to reach every goal I set.

You have everything going for you. You have youth, you have education, you are able to see life from a high perspective, and you have a great ability to express yourself and your feelings in English as well as in Chinese. These qualities will carry you far if you can keep a positive attitude toward life. If you fall into worry and discouragement, much of your energy and time will be wasted.

So, Gladys, my experience tells me that you are going to be successful and that you are on your way to leading a very productive life. Please make my prediction come true.

With warm regards and best wishes, Bob

The Open Mind

Dear Bob,

It's a great honor to write to you. I could not help but write to you because you write so well. To keep our minds open, we can often benefit from the thoughts of others. I am a teacher. I think your topics do me a good favor.

As a teacher, I should keep my mind open. Then I can be a good and wise teacher. Thanks for your thoughtful ideas.

Yours, Yu Huiling (Jiangsu)

▲

Dear Huiling,

I always enjoy receiving letters from our readers in China, especially enjoy letters written by teachers because I believe that teaching is one of our most important professions. To be able to teach is a function that deserves the highest praise.

You write with much wisdom when you urge us to keep our minds open. A closed mind is as useless as a bicycle is to a fish.

I think of students as lamps ready to be lighted. I envy your students. They are the future, and the future depends upon fresh thinking with open minds and open hearts.

With warm regards and high hopes for a successful life of teaching, Bob

Communication

Dear Sir,

I am a college student. I like English very much. The first time I have been intrigued by an English article was when I read your January column, "Time." You wrote with a philosophical view and humor. Sir, it's you who brought me into a world filled with charming sentences and intelligent thoughts. Thank you!

Best wishes to you, Haiya (Hangzhou, Zhejiang)

▲

Dear Haiya,

Thank you for your gracious letter. You renew my confidence that we are going to have a better world. Please keep up your spirits and remember that optimism is a gift that we share.

With best wishes, Bob

▲

Dear Mr. Herman,

After reading the article, "The Universe," in your column in *Overseas English*, I feel relaxed, and my mind has suddenly become bright and broad. I think that your words are full of wise thoughts. I love them so much. I love the last sentence, "Let's keep asking questions even though they may not have answers," the most. Thus I was inspired to ask some questions about growing.

I was brought up in a conservative family. In the course of my growing up, my parents often told me many "shoulds and should nots." I am very uncomfortable with this way of teaching, and I hate it. Although my parents are good and honest, they don't understand me at all. I put much effort into communicating with them before I turned 21 years old, but I failed over and over again. They do not listen to me. I want to talk to them less and less. I am 24 and believe that it is impossible to communicate frankly with my father. I usually feel extremely sad about this. Why is it so difficult to have good communication between children and parents? Many families in China have the same problem. How can we solve it?

I expect to hear your answer. Thank you!

Sincerely, Ivy (Yichang, Hubei)

▲

Dear Ivy,

I am deeply touched by your letter. I am grateful for all my Chinese readers and for their opinions.

Many of us, like you, were brought up in conservative families, and we spent much of our earlier lives listening to "shoulds and should nots." I wonder if our parents grew up the same way with their parents telling them what they should and should not do?

This is what we call the "generation gap," and it does sometimes become a "veneration gap." This is sad, and there must always be time to speak to each other about this gap and to get each other to understand the many ways the world has changed from one generation to another.

Of course we must always respect our elders and try to understand how hard it is for them to accept the many changes that are taking place daily. You ask how to settle this poor communication between children and parents. Every family is different. In many cases it is best merely to accept the fact that there is no way to "educate" your parents and try to avoid all confrontations. Argument often leads to anger, and anger hurts everyone involved. My guess is that your parents have lived the lives that they feel are honorable and successful and productive. Please never question this. They feel protective toward you, and it is probably painful for them to see you going into a world that is becoming more and more foreign to them, a world of changing values and manners. This is very common in America and apparently also in China.

After giving deference to your parents and accepting their concerns, you must follow your own heart and mind. Your life is your responsibility and, at the age of 24, no longer the responsibility of your parents. It is true that many children can be harmed unwittingly by parents who desire to guide and protect them.

One of the secrets of success in life is self trust. This requires our confidence in ourselves, knowing that we may make mistakes, but that these will be our own mistakes and we will learn from them. Each of us at some time must free ourselves from parental control. In the best of worlds, we can convince our parents of this wisdom. I hope you will be able to. Please try. Parents often want control, whereas children want freedom. Control and freedom do not mesh well with each other.

I believe that your writing to me shows that you have made a good start. You are able to explain your situation to me and to yourself. There is an old proverb which tells us, "He who is outside his door has a hard part of his journey behind him." You seem to be "outside the door." Excellent! Stay outside the door. This is your big first step, but also keep the door open so that your parents will be proud of you and all that you are doing with your freedom.

Again, thank you for confiding in me. The length of this response shows how much I care about your situation and how much I feel you are on your way to a successful life.

Respectfully yours, Bob

Dear Editor,

Thank you for your instant reply! I was very happy to receive Bob's and your letters. If you think my letter is helpful to other readers, you can publish it. Thanks.

Could you translate the sentence in Bob's letter, "He who is outside his door has a hard part of his journey behind him," in Chinese for me? I cannot completely understand it. Thank you.

Best wishes, Ivy (Yichang, Hubei)

▲

Dear Mr. Herman,

I was surprised to get your response so quickly! I am very thankful for your opinions! Your words are reasonable. They have woken me up from a dream.

Parents are always prepared to protect and control their children out of concern. The "generation gap" has remained in many families. What I need to do is to take care of my parents and to satisfy them. I know there are some questions in the world without given answers. I only wish my efforts could make my father happy and that all parents and children in this world would care for each other in order to make everyone happy.

Could you recommend books on English culture to me? Thank you again for your help.

Sincerely yours, Ivy (Yichang, Hubei)

▲

Dear Ivy,

The phrase, "He who is outside his door has a hard part of his journey behind him," is like the old Chinese proverb which tells us that, "The longest journey begins with a single step." When we venture outside, it is that first step which is the hardest to take. After that we are free to pursue our journey.

I am pleased that you wish to read books on English culture. I suggest that you consult either your library or bookstore for recommendations.

I admire your attitude toward your parents. Sometimes they seem out of step with the times, but they do have an accumulation of experience which can be of benefit to you. I feel sure that they will eventually feel proud of you, and will be pleased to watch you succeed in your life's journey.

Respectfully yours, Bob

Failure

Dear Mr. Herman,

I like to read your column. From it, I understand more, and it is good not only for my studies but also for my life.

I am a high school senior. I am busy studying and preparing for the most important examination of my life. It is my only way to get into my dream university, but it is very difficult for me. I know I have so many disadvantages. Though I always try my best to overcome them, they are still present.

Recently, I had a midterm, but I didn't do well. I have had several failures. My friend always gets good grades on her exams. I envy her so much. I even want to give up. The future is unknown for me. I want to do well in everything, and I remember the proverb, "No pain, no gain," but why does my pain never gain what I expect? I want to hear your advice very much. Thank you.

Sincerely yours, Jennifer

▲

Dear Jennifer,

You seem to be such a bright, thoughtful young woman. From your letter you seem to have lost confidence in yourself. You are too young to feel disappointed. Each of us has a holy spark within us, and this spark is called "life." This is a gift given to you at birth, and you must use it carefully. Don't waste it in doubt!

We are told that what does not destroy us makes us stronger. You have not been destroyed, so use your disappointments to make you stronger. You write about your "failures." A feeling of failure can erode your strength the way that water can wear away rocks. You can't let disappointments or failures distress you. The important thing is never despair!

One of my favorite African proverbs tells me that, "To lose your way is one way of finding it." This means that we have to learn from our mistakes and our failures rather than be distressed over them.

Jennifer, please get on with your life and stop wasting energy by feeling sorry for yourself. This is what we call a "cop out." Every one of us is responsible for finding our purpose in living. From your letter, I can tell that you have a mission. You have no disadvantages, only advantages. Keep your attention on these, and stop fretting over minor complaints.

Please keep your thoughts on the "big picture," and I know that you are heading for success in your life.

Respectfully yours, Bob

Higher Education

Dear Bob,

Now that I have heard from the colleges I applied to, I have to make my decision in less than a month. I can't seem to decide between the University of California at Berkeley and the University of Pennsylvania. My dad really wants me to go to Berkeley because it is much less expensive to attend and closer to home. However, Pennsylvania's business program is ranked higher, and I have always wanted to live in the East. Unfortunately, I haven't visited either college, so it is difficult to predict which school I would be happier at.

I really don't want to make the wrong choice, since I know this decision will affect the rest of my life! Any advice would be greatly appreciated.

Thanks in advance!

Sincerely, Jenny

▲

Dear Jenny,

I hasten to respond to your note. I understand your confusion about making a choice between Berkeley and Penn, and the advantages of each. These have to be weighed carefully before making a choice, and you probably will never know if your choice was the best one. This is what makes life so interesting.

There are several factors to be considered in this choice. I am aware of only a few. These would be (in no order):

- The quality of each college. (It's academic standing)
- What specifically the college will offer to you. (Perhaps in finance courses)
- The relative expenses.
- The impact of each on your family relationships.
- Your personal desires. (Where friends might be, weather change, commuting time, prestige, etc.)

I think that the decision has to be yours in conjunction with your mother and father. From a distance, I feel that the national ratings mean very little. The differences between these two choices are not relevant. In the future no one is going to say you went to number 4 or number 1 or number 30. The future will depend on how you are able to adjust to the school environment and on several elements of luck which you cannot predict (roommate, faculty, friendships, etc.).

Regarding family considerations, which are tied to financial costs, being away from home, accessibility, and other emotional factors, these are very personal and I am not able to comment on with any intelligence.

One suggestion would be this: Since you are trying to decide between two unknowns, would it be possible to visit either or both over the coming months? This would give you a much better basis for deciding. Colleges usually prefer that applicants visit them, attend a few classes, see what the living conditions are, and get a general sense of the campus and the opportunities that exist outside the campus.

Perhaps you could visit Berkeley with Mahya. This is not such a long trip, and you could notify them that you will be visiting. Philadelphia is further away. Mahya tells me that she and Trent may be visiting New York in early May. If it is important enough for you, could you arrange to go with them and make a side trip to Philadelphia?

I am suggesting this based only on my own personal experience. I was trying to decide among Dartmouth, Penn, and Union. I visited all three and the decision became very clear after I visited each. Of course this was in 1937, and much has been changed since then.

Jenny, please don't over worry this. I am typing thoughts quickly as they come into my head. I do wish you could see (and feel) both campuses before deciding. You will be successful in either, yet a choice has to be made. There are advantages to each. Berkeley is less expensive and closer to home for visits. The weather is more accommodating. It would make your father happier. Penn is in Philadelphia which I imagine would be a more exciting environment than Berkeley. Academically I would rate them even—both top colleges.

One more thought: If you are inclined toward Berkeley (or to Penn), you could try it for a year and if some of your hesitations proved correct, you could transfer to another college.

Let's stay in touch. You are smart, beautiful, sensitive, and charming. Either college will be privileged to have you.

With love, Bob

Dear Bob,

Thanks so much for your wise advice. It gave me much to think about, so I am still trying to decide which college to attend. Now that I realize how important this decision is, I am even more hesitant to choose.

I think I am leaning towards Penn, but my dad still wants me to go to Berkeley, and I do not want to disappoint him. This is so difficult; I really don't know what to do. What do you think I should do?

Sincerely, Jenny

▲

Dear Jenny:

Please be sure that whichever college you decide upon will be the best for you. If you still have your heart somewhere else, there will be time to consider a transfer later.

The important choice you face is to understand how privileged you are to be able to attend either Berkeley or Penn. This is a choice that is denied to millions of young persons here in America, in China and in every other country.

Entering college must be one of the most exciting periods in our lives. A new environment, new responsibilities, freedom from parents, independence of thought, new friendships, access to learning, new problems of adjustment, everything new and different. How exciting and how welcoming! Yet there is the same Jenny, bright, eager to learn and to laugh, wanting to face all these new responsibilities and all the innovations, confident of her ability to greet and meet change.

Jenny, all this newness will be like a fresh breeze sweeping through your life. Every challenge will provide a breath of freedom (and responsibility). Breathe deeply, use your mind and your heart as well as your lungs, keep your head high, know that we love you, and enjoy.

Gosh, I do sound like Mr. Landers, but I feel so much love for you and I have so much confidence in you that I have to "let it all out" in this letter.

Let's stay in touch. With love, Bob

▲

Dear Bob,

Thanks again for sharing your thoughts! I have finally decided; I am going to Penn!

Thank you for helping me throughout the entire college process: letters of recommendation, advice before interviews, support during the stressful week when I was hearing back from colleges, advice for choosing my college, and wisdom that always reminds me to keep things in perspective. Thank you for your invaluable friendship!

Sincerely, Jenny

Persistence

Dear Bob,

I am from Changchun University, and my major is in Business Administration. My dream position is a CEO, and I would also like an MBA degree. Now I'm a junior, and I lead a busy life.

Thank you for your last story about a Harvard MBA businessman. It indeed gives me tips on what a real life is, but I still believe that to strive for one's aim requires much courage. I admire you so much, because even at the age of 83, you still devote your heart and soul to learning and teaching. May you have even more success! I am expecting your precious advice!

Jhon (Changchun, Jilin)

Dear Jhon,

I enjoyed reading your letter. Congratulations on your work toward becoming a CEO. This is a fine ambition. I admire you for working toward an MBA, which is an important first step. To have a definite aim in life and to use one's energy in striving to reach it are twin gifts. I wish more persons had goals and had the courage to work to achieve them.

In order to really understand a person, we need to know not only what he has done but also what he intends to do. Please continue to keep your goal in mind. I believe that you have the courage and the persistence to achieve whatever you wish. When you become CEO, please let me know the name of the company so that I can follow your career.

With best wishes and warm regards, Bob

The Planet

Dear Bob,

I write this letter to you with respect.

As your reader and translator, I like your essays very much. You use simple words to express deep thoughts and philosophical ideas. I believe that you are doing a lot of good for your readers. Through reading your wit and wisdom stories, they will try their best to be kind and merciful with noble hearts.

All the best wishes to you. I hope that your life tree will be green forever.

Yours sincerely, Liu Jiaqi (Tanjin)

P.S. Here is my photo. I hope that I can receive yours in return.

▲

Dear Jiaqi,

Mahya sent me your letter and photo. Thank you very much for both. They are treasures that I shall cherish.

Your smile is very attractive. Every time I look at it, I smile back.

Your words concerning my articles are very warm and thoughtful. They are probably too complimentary. I write quickly, whatever my feelings tell me to write. I believe that if enough of us can share our hopes and feelings with each other, there should be no room for hostility. We must learn to give dignity and respect to everyone. If we do, I believe that the dignity and respect will be returned to us.

Life is too brief to be nasty. Because we share the same earth home, we must agree to make it a better place to live and work in. There is no alternative that makes any sense to me. This is not a message; it is an imperative.

Thank you again for your kind remarks. I am pleased that you are translating our book. Mahya tells me such wonderful things about you and about your ability to translate. Thank you again for all your work.

I will ask Mahya to send you my photo. It is not a very recent one, but it is the only one I have.

With warm regards and best wishes, Bob

▲

Dear Bob,

I read your column today in the May issue of *Overseas English*. After reading it, I was deeply moved by your kind words and warm encouragement. You are not only our wise teacher but also our best friend.

There is a poem written by our famous ancient Chinese poet, Du Fu. In the poem, he wrote, "Good rain knows season, it nourishes everything in silence." It reminds me of your articles and letters. They are just like such rain.

One European philosopher once said that thoughts growing from a dove's feet would dominate the whole world. It is a pity that he said it too early. Our earth is not calm. War breaks out here and there, but I do believe that friendship, love, and kindness are to replace hostility, hatred, and cruelty.

The beautiful dream of all sensible men will come true eventually. Of course, we must make an effort to shorten the distance between dream and reality.

It's an honor to live on the same globe and in the same century as you do. Life may be brief, but friendship, love, and the beautiful dream will last forever.

Best wishes for your career.

Your friend, Lu Jiaqi (Tianjin)

▲

Dear Jiaqi,

It was a special pleasure for me to read our correspondence in *Overseas English*. We must thank Mahya for putting this together. She is a very special person, and she has a special fondness for you. This makes three "specials" in one paragraph!

Yes, we must shorten the distance between dream and reality as you suggest. Both are important. Without dreams, we are not much above the other animals. And without reality, we are nothing.

You mention the need to replace "hostility, hatred, and cruelty." This is necessary in order to gain peace in our troubled world. I would add the need to eliminate poverty. Poverty is a menace to our civilization. One of the "facts" of modern life is that we have the resources to eradicate poverty, and that we are using these resources for other purposes.

Starvation and malnutrition exist in many parts of this world. This is a disgrace. It is hard to believe that privileged persons can avoid feeling guilty over this deplorable situation.

Beyond the basic needs for food, shelter, and clothing, I would define poverty as the lack of adequate income, health, education, and housing. These are necessary ingredients for successful living in today's complex society. We are told that things which matter most should never be at the mercy of things which matter least. It is this "opportunity" gap which must matter most to all of us, especially to those of us who are the most privileged.

It was Winston Churchill who mentioned the "unnatural gap between the rich and the poor." In many parts of the world this gap is growing rather than diminishing. It threatens our stability and our moral sense. Allowing poverty to exist around us is a shame. The poor and the weak need the help of the rich and the powerful. This must be a requirement of every modern society.

Of course there are other forms of poverty. These include the poverty of ideas, the poverty of understanding, and the poverty of compassion for our fellow human beings and for our natural environment. These we will reserve for future comment.

Thank you again for your letter. You see what an outflow of words you have inspired.

With great respect and best wishes, Bob

P.S. Thank you again for translating my articles. This has been a twin blessing for me. I have found a warm friend in addition to a fine translator.

Self-Consciousness

Dear Mahya,

During an evening study session in the classroom, I tried my best to pay attention to my math book. Some of our classmates often talk with each other, so I couldn't help but watch them and listen to their conversation. There were more than three beautiful girls. Even though I know them, I hardly talk to them.

I want to talk with girls, but I don't know how to start. I'm a shy boy, but I believe I will talk with those girls someday.

By the way, it is normal not to pay attention when studying, because the term has just begun. What do you think? What did you do during your vacations?

Best wishes to you.

Yours, Johe (Chongqing)

Dear Johe,

Thank you for writing to me. I want to try to be sad for you, but I am not able to. I envy your youth and your ability to study and to learn. You are in a wonderful stage of your life. To be able to watch "three beautiful girls" is a joy that many of us do not have.

Being shy is common for boys of your age. I was probably more shy than you when I was your age, but I found that girls like shy boys more than they like aggressive boys. These girls probably wish you would speak with them. Maybe you could just ask the beautiful girls if they like shy boys? This might be a good introduction and a good start for you.

Johe, when I was your age, I was told that the great purpose of life is not knowledge, but action. I hope you will combine the two—girls and study. I think you will find the combination very pleasing. I did. To answer your question, this is how I spent my vacations when I was at the University.

With best wishes for success with both study and girls, Bob

Friendship

Dear Bob and Mahya,

Thank you for your advice.

My friendship is in trouble. I have a friend who used to live with me in the same dorm. He gradually distanced himself from me and suddenly told me that I was no longer his friend.

There is a popular saying in China: "Something smells good from far away, but bad when close by," but it's wrong in friendship. Therefore, I wrote this letter to you with hopes of getting advice. Did you ever experience anything like this?

Yours, Johe (Chongqing)

Dear Johe,

In writing to you, I neglected to emphasize how important study is to your future. If you study extra hard, you might get a big job, and if you are successful in this big job, you might become popular, and if you become popular, the beautiful girls will come to you. This might be one of the best routes to them! What do you think?

Keep faith in yourself.

Best, Bob

P.S. I just received your second letter telling me about your friend. It is not easy to lose a friend. If you are not able to persuade him to change his mind, this may be an opportunity for you to seek new friends. Of course it would be helpful to you if you could find out the reason why he left you. Sometimes human relations can be repaired, but first we must know the reason they were impaired.

Keep your faith in yourself and in others, Johe, and your life will be a happy one.

With best wishes, Bob

Responsibility

Dear Bob and Mahya,

Thank you for "We Learn and We Laugh Together" in *English Salon*. I still remember, "You got to walk that lonesome valley. Nobody else can walk it for you. You got to walk it by yourself." It's a good proverb.

My mother, grandma, and grandpa live in my home. My mother sells shoes for a living. She is more than forty years old. In the future, the responsibility for my family will be on my shoulders. It's a heavy task, but I have to accept it. It's a street on which I have to walk alone.

Best wishes to you.

Faithfully yours, Johe (Chongqing)

Dear Johe,

I am impressed by your feelings and by your understanding. This is a strange world, yet it is the best one that we have. We do walk alone, yet we are all together. We all share the same needs for food, for shelter, for clothing, and for love and inspiration. Yet each of us has an individual personality. No two minds or bodies or hearts are the same.

I admire your feelings about your parents and grandparents. You (and I) are parts of a chain. This chain can bind us to the past, or it can keep us from unwinding in the present. Please continue to think and to feel and to work.

With warm regards and best wishes, Bob

Dear Bob and Mahya,

Thank you for your letters. Please tell me something about Bob. I have learned a lot from Bob, but too little to really know him. I know that Bob is busy with all the letters from China, but I do not know about Bob's life, his dreams, his hobbies, and his family. Mahya, can you tell me about them? Please tell me his stories.

Thank you, Mahya. With warm regards and best wishes.

Yours faithfully, Johe (Chongqing)

Dear Johe,

Thank you for writing to us again. Thank you for asking me about Bob. I would be happy to tell you more stories about Bob if we could meet in person.

Dr. Herman is a passionate, generous, and humorous person. He describes himself as "a sometimes executive, author, economist, educator, humorist, and sometimes none of these." Let me tell you about "none of these."

Bob and his wife, Beatrice, live in Slingerlands, New York, a village about two hours away (by train) from New York City. They have two sons, Arthur and Gerald, and three grandchildren, Benjamin, Emily and Katie.

Cultivating a vegetable garden, playing tennis, and riding a bike are a few of Bob's hobbies. I cannot describe these for you because I have never been to his Slingerlands home. He has two other hobbies: collecting cartoons and playing ping pong.

(I just visited Bob's home last week. In his study room, filled wall-to-wall with books, Bob and I spent hours reading e-mails from China and sending e-mails to China. His hometown is very quiet and peaceful, and his cozy home is filled with many lovely souvenirs from all over the world. It was my great pleasure to pay Bob and Beatrice a visit. What a nice treat!—Mahya 5/14/2003)

I have played ping pong with Bob and his two sons. I lost to Gerry and then to Arthur. "Winning against their dad may bring me some confidence," I reminded myself when Bob and I had a challenging game last week, before he headed to New York. When our score reached 20-20, Bob said to me, "Let's stop here. I like the 20-20. We are real partners." He did not win against me; instead he gave me a hug.

Everyone in our ping pong club likes his sense of humor. Once he wrote to me, "I find that winning is not as fun as losing. By losing a game, you are making more friends." I have thought about this. I do like to win, but it is true that when you lose you are making your opponent happier.

You asked me what Bob's dreams are. I am guessing that his dreams are to serve others, especially those less fortunate than himself, and to make the world a better place to live in.

Dr. Herman has become well-known in China. Each day, he reads e-mails from Chinese readers. Reading and writing e-mails has become a part of his daily life. "Is there anyone left in China who hasn't written to us?" he jokes. His wit and wisdom have touched many lives.

Jenny, my 17-year-old daughter, often e-mails Bob and asks for advice. His responses have enriched her life and helped her gain a better understanding of our big world as well as her small world. One day, Bob and Jenny talked for over an hour when Bob and Beatrice came to our house for lunch. Jenny understands that she is lucky to have a close friend like Bob.

Here is an e-mail I received this morning:

Dear Friends,

Most of us miss out on life's big prizes. The Pulitzer. The Nobel. Oscars. Tonys. Emmys. But we're all eligible for life's small pleasures. A pat on the back. A kiss behind the ear. A four-pound bass. A full moon. A smile. An offer of help. An empty parking space. A crackling fire. A friendly e-mail. A great meal. A glorious sunset. Hot soup. Cold beer. Don't fret about copping life's grand awards.

Maybe we should enjoy its tiny delights? Bob

It brightened my day. I hope it will have the same effect on yours, Johe.

Bob is a unique gentleman with wisdom, compassion and courage. I am very pleased that he has brought more happiness to China. I have been so fortunate to be considered one of Bob's many friends; learning and laughing with Bob has added years to my life. I know he will impact even more lives in the future.

Best wishes, Mahya

▲

Dear Bob and Mahya,

Thanks, Mahya, for telling me about Bob.

Bob is fond of playing tennis, and so am I. His words are great: "Let's stop here. I like the 20-20. We are real partners." There is no doubt that Bob has a vast heart.

I can picture when Jenny and Bob were talking. Isn't that sweet? I was surprised because my friends and I hardly talk to any persons who are Bob's age. Maybe there is a generation gap. Our parents always repeat the same words to us, which we can even recite. Mahya, I hope that you know how I feel. However, it is interesting to talk with Bob and you. I cannot help writing to Bob and you, because you two are very appealing.

Faithfully yours, Johe (Chongqing)

✦

Dear Bob and Mahya,

I am having trouble with my roommates. One is always angry with me, and he uses bad words when arguing with me. The other one refuses many of my invitations and suggestions. He has made some new friends and spends time with them instead of with me. The distances between my roommates and me grows longer and longer.

I want to have good friends, so I have to think about these things seriously.

I look forward to your letter.

Yours sincerely, Johe (Chongqing)

✦

Dear Johe,

I would enjoy meeting your friends. They seem to be very different from each other. They certainly present different problems for you.

Being an ocean away, and not knowing either of these gentlemen, I am not able to comment on the questions you raise. Just remember, Johe, that most of life consists of relationships. How we treat these relationships will determine the kind of life we lead. You seem to be a thoughtful person, and you seem to be taking your relationships seriously. This is a good start.

Please tell your friends that I think they are fortunate in having you as a friend.

With best wishes, Bob

Dear Johe,

I read Bob's letter, and I admire his patience and kindness. Please take all of his advice seriously.

Have you shared Bob's column with your roommates? If you haven't, please do so today. Bob's words have changed many people's minds and even their lives, and I am sure sharing Bob's beautiful thoughts will refine the relationships between you and your roommates.

I was told that you have to find out what's wrong with yourself if you cannot get along with two or more people. Very often, I use this "mirror" to adjust my relationships with others, and it is very helpful. Would you like to give it a try?

Best wishes for a happy college life, Mahya

▲

Dear Bob and Mahya,

Thank you, Bob, for replying to my letter. Thank you, Mahya, for your advice. I told my classmates about your column, "We Learn and We Laugh Together."

The "mirror" mentioned in Mahya's letter has helped me and made me aware of the differences between my friends and me. Why can one of my roommates get along well with his friends but not with me? I have noticed that his friends don't tell him what he should and shouldn't do. The "mirror" method is useful! Now my roommate and I are improving our relations through our shared hobby—badminton. He even invited me to meet his parents at his home, and I got to know more about him. I am very happy, and my heart is filled with joy.

I am still having problems with my other roommate, but I will solve them someday. I believe that I will be successful.

Sincerely yours, Johe (Chongqing)

Lifestyles

Dear Bob,

I found your article very good and helpful. I am a junior at Anhui University of Science and Technology in Anhui province. Many of my classmates are preparing for the graduation exam, and I am too. Because of this, I give up much of my time. I don't have a girlfriend, and I haven't considered it because I don't think I have time.

The problem is that some girls laugh at me and say I am abnormal. I don't know what to do. Can you give me some advice?

Best regards, Johpkson (Hefei, Anhui)

▲

Dear Johpkson,

Thank you for asking my advice. I admire your seriousness about your studies at university. It is not possible for me to help you decide how to apportion your time between your studies and girls. This is a highly personal decision.

Each of us has a personal lifestyle, and these lifestyles change as we change and have new experiences. Whether you have a girlfriend or not should be entirely your choice. You certainly are not "abnormal." Every one of us is unique and should be responsible for how he wishes to spend his time and energy. We must respect our individual differences. If girls laugh at you, this is their problem, not yours! It is good that we are not all alike. What a dull world that would be!

Johpkson, just follow your own bliss and brush aside all these petty criticisms. Being a good student at university is a fine achievement. Keep at it.

With best wishes and respectfully yours, Bob

Dear Bob,

I was very happy to receive your letter, and I have more self-confidence now. Thank you.

I know college life is especially important in one's life. Life is short; there is no excuse for us to waste it. In your article, you mentioned something about that. My classmates and I enjoy reading it. We hope for more.

Best regards for your work, and I hope you are happy every day.

Johpkson (Hefei, Anhui)

Beggars

Dear Bob,

I read your column, "Adventures of the Mind." I like it very much.

I have a question. I often meet beggars on the street, but I'm afraid to walk by them. I don't know if they are real beggars. Have you ever been in this situation? What do you think of them? If you were, what would you do?

Yours, Kelly (Jiaozuo, Henan)

▲

Dear Kelly,

I am pleased that you like my column. I enjoy writing them.

The question you raise is a common one, and we have it in America too, especially in our large cities. Beggars, like the rest of us, are much different from each other. Some are honest, others dishonest. Some can be trusted, others cannot. Some may even be harmful, the vast majority is not. Some are lazy, others are just poor, hungry, and desperate for help.

In the best of all worlds, there might not be a need for persons to beg, although in some religious traditions, begging is the greatest of all occupations. When begging is due to extreme poverty, I believe that we must be sympathetic and accord beggars the same dignity that we give to others who may be more fortunate.

I am not advocating anyone developing social relations with beggars. In today's complex societies, it is not wise to enter into relationships with any strangers. This is unfortunate, because we want to be open and trusting. It is a fact of modern living, however, that there are predators among us. These are persons who make a business of exploiting others.

So, in response to your question, I would advise you to be respectful to beggars, not to let yourself become involved with them, but never to look upon them with disdain.

With warm regards and respectfully yours, Bob

Teaching English

Dear Bob,

I just got an idea. I want to teach children English. When I was at school, the teacher taught us the 26 letters and phonetic symbols first, then the simple words. It was boring. Every day, we recited the words and later forgot them. It was a mechanical method.

Children are different from adults. They know nothing about English. I think that if I teach them English, I must first stimulate their interest. Also, I expect them to immediately use what I have taught them.

I'm not a teacher. I would like to find interesting ways to teach students. Please help so that children will be able to learn English happily.

With best wishes, Kelly (Jiaozuo, Henan)

▲

Dear Kelly,

I am glad that you have decided to teach children. Nothing can be more important. The lessons we teach children are the lessons they will teach the world.

Yes, as you say, children are different from adults. They tend to be more creative and less inhibited. Many of their inhibitions result from the criticisms they receive from adults. Children are in need of models, not critics. I believe that if more adults and parents understood this, our planet would be more habitable and a less dangerous place to live in.

Teaching English must be a formidable challenge in China because our languages are so different. The old fashioned way that you describe, beginning with the 26 letters, can be successful, but it can also be tedious. My experience in teaching is that the best way to begin is with some motivation, especially when we are teaching children. They must be given some reason to learn, and learning should be as much fun as possible.

You might try to begin by reciting nursery rhymes with the children. Some of the English nursery rhymes have good rhythm, and children enjoy repeating them. Telling simple short stories and having the children try to repeat them is also a fun way of beginning.

If available to you, there are many technical tools that can be helpful. Television series such as "Sesame Street" and others are available on cassette, videotape, and DVD. Drilling the 26 letters into children sounds a bit dull to me. When I began, I had to learn the alphabet over and over again. It was as exciting as watching paint dry, and as a child I could sense no connection between this and what I was hearing adults saying to each other.

Congratulations, Kelly. I hope you are successful in stimulating children to learn, no matter what the subject. The first step always is getting the children to believe in you, and for you to believe in them. Children will live up to whatever you believe in them. I admire your courage. Teaching English must require not only courage but also much patience. Please practice both.

With warm regards and best wishes, Bob

Life and Death

Dear Bob,

I'm your old friend and also your honest supporter. I am glad to take part in your column. I wrote an article, "Life and Death." Please give me advice. Thank you!

Life and Death

Once I never knew what death meant, as I never knew the meaning of life. Now I begin to fear death, as I understand the value of life.

Somebody said death, which is hateful, should be nonexistent. Life, which is beautiful, should last forever.

Surely, this is our desire.

But we must know that life and death are inseparable. They are like twins. There is life; there must be death. Life and death are the two extremes of the life process. Life is the beginning, and death is the end.

Life itself is a joy. It is a gift to be enjoyed. Men, for the sake of making a living, forget how to live.

In fact, we think life is beautiful because of the existence of death. It is because of our limited lives that we realize the need to treasure them. Each of us tries to design his life to make it more beautiful and more meaningful.

Death is not formidable. Death is not a period but a comma in the story of life.

If we live truly, we shall truly live.

If you want to have a happy life, remember two things: In matters of principle, stand like a rock; in matters of taste, swim with the current.

The vigor of life makes a better world.

Sincerely, Kelly (Jiaozuo, Henan)

Dear Kelly,

Thank you for sending me your article, "Life and Death."
These are the two most important events that comprise our
human experience. I am impressed by your thoughts and the
beautiful way you express them. Every day, I learn from the
letters I receive from our Chinese readers. Your letter will stay
with me as long as I live.

Your comments on Life and Death are profound, and
they are elegantly expressed. All of us, every human being
and every animal, are living life and approaching death at the
same time. I am convinced that we must try to understand
both. Without life, there would be nothing. Without death,
there would be no renewal. In terms of a popular American
song, "We can't have one without the other."

The fear of death is understandable. It is so "final," and
we are not accustomed to finality. The death of friends robs
us of their friendship. Our own death robs us of the time we
would like to have in order to continue our life's work.

The denial of death is common throughout the world.
It forms the basis of many religions and beliefs about karma
and reincarnation and other forms of afterlife. We see this
in tombs which were built by ancient peoples. These tombs
were littered with possessions that the deceased would need
after death.

The promise of an afterlife is also used to convince people that their present oppressed life is merely temporary. Vast
populations have been told that if they are patient and submit
to authority, they will be rewarded after death.

In a way, I envy persons who believe in perpetual life, even
though it may not be on this earth. Every person deserves
respect for his (or her) view of life and death, and I would
not wish to preach my views to others. Life can be a struggle,
and each of us must struggle with it in the best way we can as
long as we are not harming others.

You express your thoughts with much sensitivity. As you
say, it is the brevity of our lives that should make us treasure
our moments more. The best advice I was given is to "be

ashamed to die until you have won some victory for humanity." I leave you with this thought.

With warm wishes and best regards, Bob

You Are Born to Fly

Dear Bob,

I read your article in the Oct. issue of *Overseas English*, and some "explanations" of love have moved me a lot and confused me greatly.

I have just broken up with my former boyfriend, who loved me a lot. He hoped to have control over me, from what I wear to what I eat, etc. The most unbearable thing was that he always suspected that I would hold affection for other boys (but the fact is that I never did).

Now I am leading a life of freedom, happiness, and independence, but I think I am not made to love, and the love (between the two sexes) does not fit me.

I can clearly be conscious of love from my parents and my friends, but maybe I am not accustomed to the love between a couple. How can this be? Does this mean that I am too young (age 18)? I am a go-getting girl, and I know what I want and what I struggle for. Am I born to fly freely, but alone?

Best wishes, Puzzled Kohli

▲

Dear Kohli,

I was delighted to read your letter. I admire your open feelings and how well you express them to me. Your letter raises such interesting and puzzling questions about love. Let me try to give you my reaction to your questions.

First, I certainly am no expert on "love." This is a word which is used too often. It is applied to so many different situations that it loses its meaning. People love their work; they love vacations; they love warm weather; they love their bicycles or their pets or their plants. We say that we love all mankind.

You raise questions over your quarrel with your former boyfriend. From what you tell me, his "love" for you was dependent upon his control over you. We often confuse love and control. Personally, I believe that when we love someone, we love the entire person, and we love him as he is, not as we want him to be.

To have control over another person means that you want to have the capability to change that person to conform to your values and beliefs. This means that your love is conditional on the other person living up to the standards that you are setting. Generally, this is not a complete love relationship, although there are millions of persons who enjoy being dependent upon others and enjoy following directions set by someone else.

Many relationships are often dictated by culture, and cultures differ all over the world. Relationships can be understood only in the context of the specific culture in which they take place.

From what you write, I believe that you do not like to be controlled, and that you prefer leading your life with greater freedom. Would you consider the following advice:

If you love something, set it free. If it comes back, it will always be yours. If it does not come back, it was never yours to begin with.

Please try to understand, however, that your desire for freedom and independence does not mean that you were not made for love. Every love relationship between two sexes is different because it depends upon the needs and the values and the personalities of each person.

Everyone defines "love" between two persons differently. To me, "true love" means the desire to give oneself to another person while at the same time being true to oneself. True love creates an "us" without destroying a "me." It is possible to give without loving, but it is not possible to love without giving. I am reminded of the words: "Love isn't love until you give it away."

True love must be reciprocal. Love can be like a fire. It can warm your heart, or it can burn your house down. It all depends on the persons involved.

From your letter and the feelings you express, I believe that you have an enormous capability for true love. Eventually, you will find just the right relationship to consummate this love, and you will demand that it be reciprocal.

You are "born to fly," as you say, and there are so many ways of flying. I feel sure that you will find the one that suits you best and that your flight will end in happiness. I have enjoyed writing to you, and remember that the heart sees better than the eye.

Respectfully yours, Bob

Perseverance

Dear Bob,

I am a college student. I am having trouble cheering myself up. It seems that it is hard to continue life on campus.

After a year of being at the university, I find that life is far what I had imagined. Every day, I have to be absorbed in heaps of work in order to pass the final exam. Doing the same thing day after day (I mean studying) is very boring. Nothing can be done to change this situation. Gradually, I am feeling more tired and withdrawn. As the saying goes here in China, "There is nothing more tragic than a heart that has died." If life goes on like this, sooner or later my heart will die. Sometimes I just want to quit. If that happens, I will be considered a coward. No one wants to be a person like that.

Please give me some advice on how to get rid of these bad feelings and how to become happy again. I would like your opinions.

Sincerely, Leonard (Beijing)

Dear Leonard,

Thank you for sharing your thoughts and worries with me. Yes, life can be brutal, and I am sure that we know of many persons who are suffering from its brutalities. I do not believe that you are one of these unfortunate ones.

You tell me that you are a college student. This, in itself, is a blessing. There are millions of persons on this planet who will envy you for the opportunity to learn and to think with others. Sure, not all college teaching is inspirational. Some of it may seem irrelevant to you. But this should be a challenge to you - to try to separate what is most important from what is less important for you to learn.

If you find studying to be boring, I find it hard to be sympathetic with you. Studying should open new paths for you. It should give you a basis for forming your opinions. It should steer you towards wanting to know more and more.

The Chinese saying that you quote is true: "There is nothing more tragic than a heart that has died." You are much too young to let your heart die. A dead heart becomes nothing. When your heart dies, you die with it. I don't think this is what you want.

You say sometimes you just want to quit, but if you do, you will be considered a coward. I think that would be an appropriate definition for any youth who thinks of quitting. Leonard, please stop feeling sorry for yourself. There is a great big world out there, and it is waiting for you to make it better. If you are a coward, you will complain about it and about your studies. On the other hand, if you are a young Chinese student at a fine university (Beijing), you will stop complaining. Instead, you will thank society for the privilege that has been given to you.

So, Leonard, stop all this nonsense about being bored. My advice is to "shape up, young man," as we say in English. Eat up your studies as if they were the finest food, and prepare yourself for a vigorous and exciting life.

You may not like my advice, but it might be of help to you if you take it seriously and follow it. I doubt that you are a coward. Cowards do not write letters to me asking what they should do. Only brave persons write, and I think you are one of these.

With best wishes and warm regards, Bob

▲

Dear Dr. Herman,

I have read your column carefully. In your article, you recounted a funny story about a duck and a pharmacist. In fact, there is a similar story in China. A rabbit went into a pharmacy three times asking for carrots. The pharmacist threatened to cut her long ears with scissors. When the rabbit went there for the fourth time, she looked around and asked, "Do you have any scissors?" "No," replied the pharmacist. "Well then, do you have any carrots?" I'm not certain whether this story stems from the story you've told. To be honest, I didn't laugh when I heard it. There is nothing humorous. Maybe it shows the different cultures between the U.S. and China.

By the way, your story about the donkey shaking off the dirt and continuing to step up is helpful to me. I love it so much that I will tell it to my friends. Thanks for your excellent work.

Sincerely yours, Leonard (Beijing)

▲

Dear Leonard,

Thank you for the letter to Bob!

I remember that Bob told us the story about the duck and the pharmacist at the ping pong club in California. After he finished the last sentence, "Do you have any grapes?" We (ages 9 to 76) all laughed out loud. Sometimes, humor doesn't have to be a big deal. Bob once wrote to me, "I find much wisdom in humor, especially if it is not taken too seriously."

Thanks for sharing Bob's column with your friends! Please watch for his future columns.

Best regards, Mahya

English Studies

Dear Sir,

I very much appreciate the chance you are giving us to communicate with you. I have a lot of questions. I hope that you can give me some advice.

I am a university student majoring in English. Although I have studied English for many years, I feel that I cannot overcome some language obstacles. I read every day, but I can't apply what I have learned from reading to the other usages of this language, especially writing. I have always dreamed of writing beautiful articles in English. However, whenever I lift my pen, I find that my words are so pale, powerless, and tedious. It is easy to learn how to speak a language, but it is hard to think in that language.

How can I improve my English? Could you please give me some advice? Thank you very much. I am looking forward to your reply.

Yours sincerely, Letitia (Harbin, Heilongjiang)

▲

Dear Letitia,

You are correct in saying that English is a hard language to learn. In reading your letter, I think you are mastering it. Your use of words is excellent. I especially like your phrase: "pale, powerless, and tedious." This is a very fine use of English words. It is obvious that to excel in a foreign language, one must practice as much as possible. This means trying to read, write, and speak as often as you can.

You dream of writing "beautiful articles in English." The letter you wrote to me is a fine beginning. Please keep dreaming and writing.

With best wishes and warm regards, Bob

From an Ocean to a Teardrop

Dear Bob,

I'm a high school senior from Shantou, a coastal city in southeast China.

I've read your article in *English Salon*. I wanted to write to you because I have some opinions that are the same as yours.

I think people around the world should express and discuss their thoughts, no matter what their nationalities are or what languages they speak. As you said, "The longest distance of all is said to be from one person to another. Maybe we will be able to shorten this distance through our conversations in *English Salon*." I turned on my computer and typed out my thoughts to you, Dr. Herman, as a friend.

I have to face entrance exams beginning on June 7, and I'm worried. I like English, but I'm weak in math. The exams are approaching; what should I do?

I'm always thinking about my future. I like Africa. My classmates ask me why. They do not understand me. They consider me to be a dreamer. I like African nature and culture, from the wild Sahara to the tropics of Zaire, from the Nile River to the Congo River, from Egypt to the Ivory Coast, Côte d'Ivoire . . . Yes, and its people.

I remember when my grandfather showed me pictures which were cut from newspapers and said, "Look at the kids in the pictures. They are the same age as you." When I saw the emaciated figures and the bright and piercing big eyes, I wished I could share my pet kittens with them so that they might be happier.

I've grown up, and now I know more about Africa. I know that in those eyes, there was a fear of hunger, disease, and violence and a thirst for help. Although the kids that I saw in the pictures might now be dead from hunger, disease, or a civil war, their cry for help has never disappeared. They need help when they are in trouble. There are hands from all over the world to light flames for them. When they are in despair, there are voices to give them encouragement.

I wish I could be a part of Africa, because I love its nature and culture and because I would like to show my mercy to the poor people. I love Africa as well as my motherland, China, and I call it "Dark Africa in a Dream."

Some of my classmates think it is ugly, wild and undeveloped. I think, as a world civilization, our common responsibility is to love, to help and to care for each other. We live in order to love, and we live because of being in love.

I'm looking forward to your e-mail. Thank you.

Sincerely, Zhang Lin (Shantou, Guangdong)

▲

Dear Lin,

I hope you are successful in your entrance exams. The competition among students for university positions must be great. It is unfortunate that the demand for education in China (and in every other nation) seems to exceed the supply. This is too bad, and I hope that in the future there will be more openings at colleges and universities so that more students will be admitted. It has been said that "education is the wing with which we fly to heaven." One of the highest priorities of every culture should be the education of its citizens.

It is easy to understand that a good education in China requires more than a proficiency in English. Even though it is important to be able to read and write in different languages, we must know what we are reading and writing about. Without some meaning, words become mere sounds.

Your affection for Africa is understandable. It is the home of millions of persons, and most of the people living there are in desperate need of help. I am no expert on Africa. I have worked in only one country on that vast continent. That was in Nigeria just before the civil war over Biafra.

As you know, Africa has many different nations and cultures. South Africa and Morocco, and Zaire, and Egypt are very different countries yet all are part of Africa. Nigeria, for example, is much different from Kenya, and these two nations are different from their neighbors. Every nation has distinct problems and features of its own. They share the same continent but have a variety of histories and cultures.

From your letter, you seem to be concerned with what we call "black Africa." This part of the world has had a sad history. It was cut into odd pieces by colonial powers, such as England, France and Germany, who were competing for the rich natural resources of the region. Different African nations were formed without regard to local values or customs.

I admire your sensitivity to Africa and its problems and your desire to help the poor citizens of these nations. Your "Dark Africa in a Dream" is a fitting title for your thoughts. If your classmates are not sympathetic to your views, perhaps it is because they lack the understanding or the information that you have.

Unfortunately, poverty and despair are not limited to Africa. They are common in all parts of this world. There are different forms of poverty. There is physical poverty which means the denial of some of the basic needs for life such as food, shelter, and clothing. This is the kind of poverty in Africa that you describe so well in your letter. There are also other kinds of poverty. There is a poverty of ideas which many persons suffer from. Then there is the poverty of understanding and of compassion for others who are less fortunate than us. I believe that we are impoverished when we lack a tolerance for other persons who may live and think differently from us.

You can tell from my long response that I enjoyed reading your letter and that I am impressed by the sensitivity of your feelings. It has been said that each of us has only one wing.

And we can fly only by embracing each other. This is the lesson I learned from your letter.

My warm regards and best wishes for whatever career you choose to follow, Bob

▲

Dear Mahya,

Thank you for forwarding my letter to Dr. Herman. It's really very kind of you! When I received your e-mail, I felt that I was on top of the world, believe it or not. How happy I was!

When my parents were out, I couldn't help answering your e-mail, although they thought I was studying. I'd rather answer your e-mail than do something that is necessary.

I really hope you and Dr. Herman can both be my friends and share in my happiness and sadness.

Happy New Year!

Yours sincerely, Zhang Lin (Shantou, Guangdong)

Rapid Change

Dear Bob,

I enjoy your articles in *Overseas English*.

I live in a small village, and my parents are both peasants. They love me very much, and I love them too. I work hard at school, but I don't succeed, so my father thinks that I am doing bad things. I really do not know how to communicate with him. I need your advice. Thank you very much.

Yours respectfully, Li Linjie (Xinxiang, Henan)

▲

Dear Linjie,

I am pleased that you read my articles in *Overseas English*. The problem that you mention is very common in America as well as in China. Both our nations are going through rapid change. The rate of technological and social change seems to be increasing. These changes are affecting all our relationships, especially the relationships between generations.

Your father probably grew up under very different circumstances from you. His lifestyle, his social attitudes, his values, and his relationships are all the result of the period in which his life was formed. You must try to understand his ambitions for you and his love for you.

Sometimes it is not easy to communicate over this "generation gap." Would it be possible for you to try to spend some time together with your father in a quiet conversation? You might discuss your different attitudes and the reasons for them. Maybe you can convince him that your generation has to go in its own direction, even though you understand that his direction was good for him.

Very often fathers do not know how to show their love for their sons. They want to, but they are unable to communicate their real thoughts. Your success at school may be dependent on the emotional support that you are able to get from your father. You might even try to tell him this.

The fact that you wrote to me about this problem of communication tells me that it is draining your energy and that you are worried over it. If it would help you, please feel free to read this letter to your father. Tell him that millions of fathers in every nation are having similar problems with their sons, and that you and he are going to be some of the first to work them out together.

Your letter is not an easy one to respond to. This is especially true because I have never met either you or your father. I wish I could be with you when you speak to him. Please give him a big **hug** for me. Tell him I am proud of you because you are trying to share your love with him, and that you hope to gain his full support for whatever you are doing in life.

Best wishes and warm regards, Bob

Dear Bob,

I read your article, "Peace," in the April issue of *Overseas English*. It is very good and has been helpful to me.

Is there any way we can know in advance what topics you will be writing about in future issues?

Yours respectfully, Li Linjie (Xinxiang, Henan)

▲

Dear Linjie,

I am happy that you are able to relate to what I have been writing for *Overseas English*. It is not possible for me to give you a schedule of future articles because this keeps changing. I select topics with two considerations in mind: (1) What do I feel comfortable writing about, and (2) what do I think will be of interest to our readers in China? Sometimes Mahya, my editor, will change priorities according to changes in world events or various other considerations.

Keep reading, writing, and thinking.

Respectfully yours, Bob

Laughter

Dear Bob,

Hi! I love *English Salon*! I am Lisa from Kunming, a beautiful city in Yunnan province. I feel so lucky to be able to read your column and to have conversations with Bob.

Mahya, I am a tour guide in Yunnan. I like English very much. It seems like a gift from God that I can talk with Bob. His column is an excellent way to make friends and to practice English. Oh, cool!!!

Bob and Mahya, I like your English, especially your humor. I will be the tour guide for foreigners during the Spring Festival. Would you please give me some humorous stories to use. Thank you so much!

Lisa (Kunming, Yunnan)

Dear Lisa,

It was a joy to read your letter and to know that you are a tour guide in Yunnan. If I am ever in Yunnan, I will ask for you to be my guide. In the meantime, I am happy that you are learning so much English. To be fluent in both Chinese and English will be a big asset to you.

Yes, it will be a pleasure to talk with you, as you suggest, through *English Salon*. I am glad that you like humorous stories. I do too. I hope you will find many of these in my columns in *English Salon*.

We enjoy life more when we can learn and laugh together. Mahya and I spend many hours together learning and laughing with each other. We are happy to know that you will be learning and laughing with us through my columns.

With warm regards and best wishes, Bob

Cultures

Dear Bob,

How is everything going? I am Lucille from Dalian!

I appreciate your articles published in *Overseas English*. It is a good way to reflect on the differences between our two cultures.

I would like an English name, and I hope you can help me. The name Squirrel was given to me as a child. Lucille is a later one. I would like a unique one. If you have any, please tell me.

Your reply will be highly appreciated.

Best regards, Lucille (Dalian)

▲

Dear Lucille,

You are right. It is important for every country to try to understand the culture of other countries. I hope we are doing this in *Overseas English*.

You ask me to suggest an English name for you. This is a matter of personal choice. Some of the names I like are Sarah, Beatrice, Lisa, Katie, Emily, Anne, Jenny, and Nancy. Of course, there are many more to choose from. Whatever name you decide upon will be just the right one for you.

With best wishes and warm regards, Bob

▲

Dear Lucille,

Mahya shared your letter with me. You ask if I would explain the U.S. to you in my columns. I am glad that you are interested, but I do not intend to write about America with all its benefits and all its faults. This I leave to travel agents and political commentators. Instead, my columns are on subjects that I believe to be of mutual interest. We do want to learn together and to be able to laugh together.

Of course I do write my opinions on a variety of subjects, but I urge my readers to consider these only my opinions and not those of an average American. I believe that we are all residents on the same earth, and I write only as one of these concerned residents.

Thank you for your interest. Bob

Self-Esteem

Dear Bob,

It is nice to meet you through *English Salon*. It is the first time that I have written to a professor whose native language is English.

I am very interested in English. I keep studying English in school and at work, but I do have confidence. At the end of November, I took an exam. To my disappointment, I failed. I am now pessimistic. Luckily, I met you. What good luck!

I hope I can hear from you soon. Would you give me your appraisal regarding my English? Thank you in advance.

Yours faithfully, Lucy (Dongguan, Guangdong)

Dear Lucy,

I am pleased that you found time to comment on my column. Your English is very good.

Please do not be discouraged because you have failed to pass one exam. It might be because the exam was not suited to you. This should be an encouragement to you to try harder for the next exam. Sometimes we learn more from an exam that we have failed than we learn from an exam that we have passed, especially if it does encourage us to try harder next time.

Reading should help you to improve your English. Also, watching English films can help you to learn conversational English.

My best wishes to you, Bob

▲

Dear Bob,

I was very glad to receive your letter so soon. Many thanks for your good suggestions.

My present job is related to English, but it is limited to written English. I am worried about my oral English. Every time I watch an English film, I can't keep up with what the actor is saying. When I talk with a foreigner or listen to the radio, I can understand what is being said because I pay attention. If someone distracts me, I get nothing. Would you tell me how to improve?

Yours faithfully, Lucy (Dongguan, Guangdong)

▲

Dear Lucy,

You are correct. English is a difficult language to hear. It is easier to read than to listen to. This is especially true because so many speakers talk rapidly and slur their words. This is the experience I have had with a number of languages. I thought I could understand Spanish and French and German because

I had studied these languages. However, when I got to these countries, I was not able to understand the spoken words like I was able to understand the written words.

My only comment to you is to continue to listen to English and to try to sharpen your ear to its inflections and pronunciation. It only requires practice.

Best wishes and good luck! Bob

Choices

Hello Bob,

I was so glad to meet you through *English Salon*, my favorite magazine. I really appreciate your attitude towards life, the soul, and spirit. I think I have learned a lot from your words.

I am an accountant at a bank. I have been working at the bank for about 10 years. I think it's very important to study English well, and I have a passion for studying the language.

Bob, do you think it's very important for a person to obtain success through his career? I do not have a passion for my job or my major. I am interested in language and psychology. I want to change my major. Is this possible at the age of 30? Many people think I am crazy. I'd like to study something that I really enjoy. I dream of going to college.

I appreciate your poem, "Damn You Memory." There are lots of memories in my life. I always keep a positive attitude.

Today is Chinese New Year. It's the biggest traditional festival in China. I give my best wishes to you during this joyful holiday. Hope to hear from you soon.

Sincerely, Lucy Liu (Chongqing)

Dear Lucy,

Thank you for your good wishes for the Chinese New Year. Mahya invited my wife and me to their home for the Chinese New Year dinner. It was a delicious meal of Chinese delicacies.

After dinner we watched the New Year celebration from Bejing via satellite. Mahya, her two daughters, Jenny and Anne, and her husband, Trent, were perfect hosts, and I felt we were really in China for the evening.

In your letter, you ask the purpose of studying. I prefer to use the term "learning" rather than "studying." Studying has many purposes. It can lead to more interesting work and sometimes to positions that are more financially rewarding. It can also enrich us by broadening our perspective on life. By reading books we gain from the thoughts and the experience of others. By studying current events we learn more about how the Universe is changing.

I admire all of your interests, especially your "passion for studying." Please do not let your friends tell you that at age 30 you are beyond studying. Learning is a lifetime occupation. I believe that every older person wishes that he had learned more. It is learning (and I would include laughing) that makes our trip through life more interesting and more rewarding.

You seem to be very successful as an accountant for 10 years. This is a fine accomplishment, and you should be proud of all that you have done. Whether you should change jobs now is a very personal decision. It is a decision which deserves careful attention. Change is often good, and continuity is often good. Sometimes the values of change and continuity compete for our attention. It would be wise to consider all the alternatives before making a decision. There must be financial aspects to a change. Then there are the personal considerations. One dominant feature of life is how we enjoy spending our time, and how productively we use our time. Time is a topic of utmost importance to everyone's life.

A career choice should take "time" into account. If you would enjoy spending your days and years doing something different, this should be an element in your decision. Another consideration is the use of your talents. Some of us are much more successful in some kinds of work than we are at others. Going to a college might help you to explore your talents and give you more opportunities to learn and to expand your horizons. It might open more choices to you.

Your positive attitude is a big step toward success, and your desire to learn more is a gift that many persons do not have. Too many persons fall into an occupational "rut" and stay in it for their entire lives. Your ambition to learn more English should also be a benefit to you.

With warm regards, Bob

▲

Mahya,

I read the letter from Bob. I understand the purpose of studying much more. I admire his sentence, "Learning is a lifetime occupation." I really appreciate his thoughts.

I think I will learn until I cannot learn one day in the future. I thought that a successful career was very important because we live in a competitive society, but after reading Bob's letter, I understand much more. The career is not all of a person. We also should focus on things that are more interesting in life.

Thank you for furthering the communication between Bob and me.

Regards, Lucy Liu (Chongqing)

Falling in Love

Dear Sir,

I'm a English teacher at No.13 Middle School. Today I read your article, "Understanding," in *Overseas English*. It touched me so much that I couldn't help writing this letter to you.

Yes, children have their own ways of viewing life, and in some ways, they know much more about life than we do, as adults. Once I was told that children don't know what is ugly. What they see is a beautiful world. It is the adults who give them the negative ideas.

When we mention love, we are likely to think of the love between males and females. In my school, we teachers are afraid of this word. There is a problem called "zao lian" (in Chinese), when students fall in love in high school. At this time, the teacher would ask them to stay away from each other.

Sometimes I don't agree with this. How do you know they are falling love? Is it because they are having lunch together? Is it so bad if they are really falling love? In my opinion, listening to the students is very important before you make a decision. What I mean by "listening to the students" is to listen to what their minds speak. Here, time is needed, and so is love. But as a teacher, I know what my colleagues worry about. We, as adults, think about responsibility more than love.

"If you bungle raising your children, I don't think whatever else you do will matter very much." What an amazing idea!

Thank you very much. Your words remind me of what is deep in my heart.

Yours, Lydia (Chongqing)

▲

Dear Lydia,

Thank you for your letter and for the wonderful sentiments that you express so well. I believe that we share many of the same thoughts regarding children and their education. Being an English teacher in a junior high school, you have valuable experience in watching children develop. I believe that those who teach children are to be even more honored than those who bear children. It is more difficult to raise children than to bear them.

Here are a few of my thoughts concerning this broad subject.

Yes, children do seem to be more creative than adults. It is a shame that they tend to lose some of their imagination as they grow and are "educated" into an adult world which emphasizes material goods and competition over some of the feelings and visions that are carried from babyhood.

We must learn to listen to children, as you point out. A classic example is that of the little girl who had just finished her first week of school. "I'm wasting my time," she said to her mother. "I can't read, I can't write—and they won't let me talk!"

Children have a simple, direct way of approaching life. They are less inhibited than adults and seem more truthful too. I am reminded of a friend who was taking pictures of a five-year-old boy and said to the boy, "You have the brightest eyes. Where did you get them?" The young boy looked at him blankly and said, "They came with my head." How direct, how honest, how uninhibited a response!

Listening to children really does not take much time, yet we seldom do. And we do ask them some rather silly questions. One of the most common (in America) is "What do you want to be when you grow up?" To a child, this is like saying, "What you are now is not enough."

Let me share this poem with you:

One hundred years from now,
It won't matter what car I drove,
What kind of house I lived in,
How much money in my bank account,
Or what my clothes looked like;
But, the world may be a little better
Because I was important in the life of a child.

I admire you and all teachers who are so important in the lives of our children. You have the future in your classrooms. This is a heavy responsibility. Nothing can be more essential in any society. How we treat our children will determine the way they will treat the world when they become adults.

I hope there are more teachers in China and in America and in all other countries who think the way you do.

With best wishes and warm regards, Bob

Miracles

Dear Bob,

After reading your Dearest letter published in *English Salon*, I considered myself so lucky for having bought this magazine. When I read your column, I immediately I had the urge to write to you. I do not know why, I just felt like testing your existence. I started to like you through the love of your words and thoughts expressed in the passage. Are you really as close to us as you say? If that is so, would you mind showing me your instant attention by replying to my letter?

Yours sincerely, Lz (Weifang, Shandong)

▲

Dear Lz,

It was a delight to receive your letter. It was written with so much enthusiasm on your part, and I reply to you with equal enthusiasm. I enjoy sharing my thoughts with readers of *English Salon*, and I always look forward to knowing what our readers are thinking about.

There is so much strife in this world. There is so much hostility between nations and between persons. I like to believe that if we can share our thoughts and our feelings with each other, we can make this planet more livable. Even though we are separated by thousands of miles, we can still communicate through magazine articles.

Thank you for taking the time to write to me. Never lose your faith in miracles. They do happen.

With best wishes and warm regards, Bob

▲

Dear Bob,

I was so excited to receive your immediate reply. Now I believe you are true to us.

Thanks for your precious time and your wonderful words. I do appreciate your encouragement. I am working hard and looking forward to miracles.

Warmest regards, Lz (Weifang, Shandong)

Pen Pals

Dear Robert S. Herman,

I am a faithful reader of yours. Thank you for your wonderful articles. I like them and learn a lot from them. I translate them into Chinese and share them with my students. They also like your articles a lot.

In college, my classmates and I had pen pals in America. I learned a lot from this.

Now I am a middle school teacher with 97 students. My students are eager to become friends with students in America so that they can learn from each other. You are the only one I know in America. Could you help me?

My students can use computers at school. It will be easy for the students in both countries to exchange their ideas. It would be very kind of you if you could help me.

I will be very thankful for your early answer.

Mel (Jiaxin, Zhejiang)

▲

Dear Mel,

Letters like yours become an important part of my life. There is no greater delight than knowing that my articles are reaching teachers and students in China. It is a privilege to know that you are taking the time to translate these articles and that they are part of your curriculum.

It is so important for all of us to communicate with each other. Life consists mostly of relationships, and the basis of relationships is communication. This is especially important when we are separated by miles of ocean and by centuries of tradition and history. Your suggestion for a stream of correspondence between students of China and America is a splendid one. I am eager to help you to do this.

Young persons can learn much from each other. They can form a bridge of understanding from one culture to another, and from one language to another. As you say, the computer and the Internet make it easier for students both in China and in America to exchange ideas.

Unfortunately, I am not familiar with the means of beginning such dialogues. Because I am not teaching, I have no students who might serve as pen pals to yours. I am sure that there are means of arranging for this. I am asking Mahya if she can give you advice on how to begin your proposed exchange. Mahya is my editor, my colleague, and my close friend. She has two daughters who are fluent in both Chinese and English. Mahya is closer to the American educational scene than I am and may be able to give you advice.

Thank you for sharing your thoughts with me. I admire persons like you who are helping to guide our future by encouraging students to learn.

With warm regards and best wishes, Bob

▲

Dear Mel,

Bob asked me if I could be of help.

One of my daughters is going to middle school this fall. Her school is an IB (International Baccalaureate) school. I would be happy to talk to her teacher about your request, which will definitely benefit both the Chinese and American students.

Unfortunately, there is only one week of school left before summer vacation. I won't know who my daughter's teacher is until the end of August. Please remind me if you don't hear from me in September.

Thank you for sharing Bob's wit and wisdom with your students. You must be a very wise teacher, and your students should be thankful to have you. I am proud of you. My personal goal is to encourage more people to enjoy Bob's beautiful writing as well as his unique thoughts. I appreciate your kind help. Please accept my hearty thanks.

Best wishes, Mahya

▲

Dear Bob,

Thank you for your timely answer and for referring me to Mahya. Thanks also for your kind words. I was so happy to receive your and her e-mails.

I translate the e-mails into Chinese orally. My students were yelling and jumping with excitement. I wish you could see how happy they were! They are countryside boys and girls. They never imagined that they could have pen pals in America.

I like poetry very much. For a while in college, I read English poems out loud every morning. I learned a lot from them. I'm fascinating with the beautiful words of William Blake and other great poets. You are good at poetry, too. I like your poem very much. I'd like to share more poems with you in the future, including Chinese poems.

With warm regards and best wishes, Mel (Jiaxin, Zhejiang)

Dreams

Dear Dr. Herman,

I like your articles in *Overseas English* very much. These articles moved me a lot. I'm a 14-year-old girl. I'm no longer a kid, but not yet an adult.

I want to ask you something about dreams. Everyone has his own dreams. Some dreams can be great, others can be common, but they are all dreams. I believe that a dream can change people, a dream can let people be great, but it also can let people down. I have a lot of dreams, and, of course, I hope they come true.

The word "dream" reminds me of a person I once knew. Unfortunately, I cannot remember his name. What he did was wonderful. When he was a teenager, he made a list of his dreams, more than 200 of them. When he grew up, he achieved most of his dreams. I hope I can achieve my dreams like he did.

Maybe in the future, I'll have more and more dreams, but how can I make **all** of my dreams come true? Life is changeable. The future is unknown for everyone. If I have some problems in the future, how will I face them? What should I do? Give up my dreams?

This is the first time I have written a letter to a great professor. I hope you can understand what I mean. Sometimes I cannot explain things clearly in English, but I try my best. I'm looking forward to your reply.

Yours truly, Yan Meng (Luoyang, Henan)

▲

Dear Meng,

It was a delight to read your letter. I am happy that you write about dreams. This word has two different meanings in English. We have dreams when we are sleeping. We have no control over these dreams. Sometimes we remember them when we awake; sometimes they just fade away from our lives.

The other kind of "dream" is what we hope for, or what we strive for, while we are awake. I believe these are the dreams that you refer to in your beautiful letter to me. I am pleased that you have dreams of this kind. It shows that you are alert and imaginative and that you view life as exciting. It also shows that you have visions of the future that you wish to achieve.

I often tell my friends to be careful what they wish for, because it is likely they will get what they wish for. I like to think that everyone everywhere has hopes and wishes and dreams about his future. These visions usually change as we go through life. They change as we have more experiences. Sometimes our "dreams" come true very early in our lives. Sometimes we have to wait for many years to reach our dreams.

Life is a journey that everyone travels. Our dreams form our destinations. It is the journey that is exciting, even though our destinations may change. As a young woman (or as a young girl), you should be dreaming. I am glad that you are dreaming about wonderful things that are going to happen to you on your journey through life.

So, my friend, it is wonderful to have dreams of what we wish to accomplish. However, it is also important to understand that these dreams will not become true unless we work hard to make them come true. If we spend all our time wishing, hoping, and dreaming, then we will be wasting valuable time. The important part of dreaming is our ability and willingness to take all the steps necessary to make these dreams come true. It is not enough just to dream. I am sure that you understand this. We must also understand that we must not become discouraged if all of our dreams do not come true. Dreaming is a continuing process, and we usually substitute new dreams for old ones.

Yan Meng, I am so impressed by your letter. I wish I had a 14-year-old daughter with the insights and thoughts that you have. Please keep having more dreams of your future, and please work hard to make them come true. And please understand that your dreams will be changing as you grow and change.

My best wishes to you. Bob

▲

Dear Dr. Herman,

I was very happy to read your letter. Thanks.

After reading your letter, I know that sometimes we dream, but, meanwhile, we should also put these dreams into action. Dreaming is an essential part of our lives. We can dream, but we shouldn't be living in the daydreams.

Sooner or later, everyone will choose his or her own path, and so will I. I will stick with my dreams and work hard for them, no matter what happens.

Thank you for giving me such great advice.

Yours truly, Yan Meng (Luoyang, Henan)

Proverbs

Dear Bob,

After reading your article about proverbs, I couldn't wait to write to you. I like proverbs very much, both English proverbs and Chinese proverbs. I think they can express our ideas in simple words. I have some interesting proverbs to share with you, and I hope you like them, too.

1. There is no rose without a thorn.
2. Barking dogs do not bite.
3. Bad workmen often blame their tools.
4. We never know the worth of water until the well is dry.
5. All crows are equally black.
6. Empty vessels make the most noise.
7. A near neighbor is better than a distant friend.
8. He who keeps company with a wolf will learn to howl.
9. Among the blind, the one-eyed is king.
10. You can't make a crab walk straight.
11. When the cat is away, the mice will play.
12. He who has a mind to beat his dog will easily find a stick.

Respectfully yours, Merlyn (Xian, Shanxi)

Dear Merlyn,

Thank you for the proverbs that you sent. I like every one of them. Each of these proverbs tells us much about life and contains some wisdom for us to follow. It is nice for me to know that persons in China like proverbs as much as I do. I will be adding more of mine in later columns.

Again, thank you for sharing these with me.

With best wishes, Bob

▲

Dear Bob,

Thanks for your third letter. I hope you are doing very well. I am very glad that you like the proverbs I sent you. "A joy shared is a joy doubled."

Christmas is near. Merry Christmas to you! Will you please send me more proverbs or English idioms in your next letter? I am eager to learn. Thank you very much!

Respectfully, Merlyn (Xian, Shanxi)

▲

Dear Merlyn,

Thank you for sending me another proverb. It is nice to know that we are learning from each other. In every issue of *Overseas English*, I am trying to remember to include several proverbs that have influenced my life. I treasure the ones you sent to me. I hope this is a happy holiday season for you.

With warm regards and best wishes, Bob

America

Dear Bob,

I read the letter you wrote to a reader of *English Salon* and was deeply moved by your kindness, your wisdom, and your humor. Just as you said in "Conversations with Bob," it's an adventurous journey of the mind. Although we share different cultures, we are all global partners, sharing the same planetary home.

I hope we can communicate by e-mail and learn more about each other's customs and culture. I believe that both of us will appreciate this.

I graduated from Nanjing University of Aeronautics and Astronomy in 2001. Now I work in Changan Airlines. Now, with economic reforms, China is getting closer to the rest of the world. The Chinese now drink Coca Cola, eat hamburgers, and watch Hollywood movies. It's the best proof that an ancient nation is melting into the world.

As a young man, I like American culture and history. I read about Abraham Lincoln and Thomas Jefferson when I was in high school. I'm very glad to have the opportunity to exchange my thoughts with you.

Best wishes, Mikery (Xian, Shanxi)

▲

Dear Mikery,

Your English is very good. I can tell that you have been studying for a long time. Congratulations on being a graduate of Nanjing University of Aeronautics and Astronomy. You must be an exceptionally bright student.

I like what you wrote about all of us being "global partners, sharing the same planetary home." This is so true. We are all living closely together, especially as a result of modern technology. The telephone, the jet engine, and now the computer have brought us all into the same neighborhood. I hope that our social and diplomatic skills will be able to keep pace with our technological skills.

With warm regards and best wishes, Bob

Origins

Dear Dr. Herman,

After reading your article about the recreation of the Universe, I want to write this letter to you to voice some of my opinions.

In recent years, more and more scholars see the necessity of redesigning our world. Most of them wish for a moderate reformation on the traditional, present mode of development. You are the first that I know of to consider creating a completely new world. You have inspired human beings' everlasting dream of living in a nirvana. This reminds me of an ancient Chinese poet Tao Yuanming, who depicts an ideal village where people know nothing about the substitution of one dynasty for another.

To me, human beings are foolish to hope for more and more material things. In fact, many things which are deemed necessary to their lives are not. As was pointed out by Diogenes, people think they possess things, but in fact they possess the people. I do not want to become extreme and deny our basic needs or a bit of luxury. Nevertheless, I feel that we are sometimes too obsessed with the need to "develop" faster and faster without considering the effects on the environment. Maybe one day people will want to develop a bit more slowly so that we may live peacefully with nature.

I like your ideas about the relationship between man and woman. There are too many tragedies caused by unrequited love, jilting, and betrayal. Loving a person consists of more giving than getting, more caring and sharing (as you mentioned) than possessing each other's body and soul.

I am looking forward to your comments on this.

Yours sincerely, Zhang Mingquan (Zhenjiang, Jiangsu)

Dear Mingquan,

It would be a delight for each of us to create a universe of our own, but, of course, it would result in chaos. All of our wishes, hopes, and aspirations would be merged into a gigantic dream. And if it were to come to pass, we would probably be horribly disappointed.

Many years ago, I was advised to be careful what I hoped for because I probably would get it. My article was intended to elicit a response, and I am so pleased to read your intelligent comments. On the subject of material things, you are so wise and your reference to Diogenes is so proper. Our possessions do possess us. I call these possessions "stuff." America (like so many other nations) is full of "stuff." The same applies to buildings. We build our buildings and then our buildings build us. We become beholden to all these purchases and forget that our aim in life might better be pointed toward improving our relations with others and making this planet more habitable for human beings and other natural beings. The only wealth is life and how we live it.

You are also wise to point out that faster is not necessarily better. We often quicken our pace after we have forgotten our objective. We bend to technology. When we achieve the capability of developing nuclear driven lawn mowers, I am sure we will try to market and use them. How sad! We race without knowing where we are heading. Our lives are so pumped up with competition and material achievements that we forget our mortality and our need for inner peace.

Your letter was a delight to read. I wish there were more persons like you on this combustible globe.

With best wishes and warmest regards, Bob

▲

Dear Bob,

I was very pleased to receive your reply. I will share your columns with my students. I also wish to have a deeper discussion with you about many other issues you might raise in your columns.

Thank you very much.

Yours truly, Zhang Mingquan (Zhenjiang, Jiangsu)

Time

Dear Bob,

I am very glad to write you again. Also, I am excited to discuss the topic of "Time" with you. In your poem, you compare time to a metronome that ticks our lives away. This is definitely true. However, I want to observe time from another angle. Since we are doomed to have a limited amount of time, the question becomes how we can make the most of our time. How can we give meaning to it? How can we live full lives rather than empty ones? Time exists in how we feel it exists. When we have a meaningful job to do that requires a lot of time, we do not usually feel the passing of time even though time is so precious. When we feel we have to kill time, time becomes so useless and so plentiful. Suppose we are immortal but not engaged in anything interesting. What will be the use of so much time? In a sense, it is the limitation upon time that gives meaning to life.

Best wishes to you.

Yours truly, Zhang Mingquan (Zhenjiang, Jiangsu)

▲

Dear Mingquan,

I agree with everything you write. Time gives meaning to life, as you say. Or maybe time, along with energy, is life. Time can be a friend or it can be an adversary, depending on how we treat our lives.

One of my fantasies is to stand on a corner with a tin cup in my hand, asking every passer-by to put into my cup all the unused minutes that they have no use for.

I admire your philosophical approach to our friend, "Time."

With warm regards and best wishes, Bob

Dear Bob,

Thank you so much for answering my letter so quickly. You are so devoted to your job, and you have answered so many letters from Chinese students. I really admire your sense of responsibility. I hope to learn more from you.

Thanks again. Happy New Year!

Zhang Mingquan (Zhenjiang, Jiangsu)

▲

Dear Mingquan,

Thank you for your note. It is a pleasure to know that my columns are being read and my thoughts are being shared with you. We do learn together. With letters like yours, the Pacific becomes more like a lake than an ocean.

With best wishes and warm regards, Bob

Love, Actually

Dear Bob,

When I get the *Overseas English* magazine, the first article I read is yours. I am reading your wise opinions about "Love." I feel joyful to see you mention that the most important thing in life is "to love and to be loved at the same time."

What I say in this letter will reveal the differences in love across the cultures. We Chinese used to be more shy in express-ing our love in public than Westerners. The popular romantic story about Liang Shanbo and Zhu Yingtai is often cited as an example. It is also compared to Romeo and Juliet. For about 2000 years in China, the Confucian doctrine had held firm con-trol of thoughts about love and marriage. Women were forbid-den to go out to meet men. In the story, Liang Zhu, the girl named Zhu was forced to appear as a man in order to go to school. When she fell in love with her schoolmate Liang, who was still in the dark about her gender, she still couldn't reveal her identity until Liang found her dressed like a girl in her home. Zhu's father insisted in marrying his daughter to another man. Finally, they both died of heartbreak and, as legend has it, turned into butterflies that can fly and love each other freely.

Today our Chinese youth enjoy almost as much freedom as Westerners when choosing their mates. That is why Valentine's Day is so popular in China now! However, one thing puzzles me so much—the divorce rate is getting higher and higher, and there are quite a few people who would like to have more than one wife, a legal one and an extramarital one.

Best wishes and warm regards, Zhang Mingquan
(Zhenjiang, Jiangsu)

▲

Dear Mingquan,

Thank you for writing on such an important subject. Everyone, sometime in their life, must deal with "love." I believe that love is the cause of the greatest pleasure and also the cause of the greatest anxiety that we face.

Even though I am not as familiar with Chinese history and culture as I would like to be, I am familiar with the romantic story, Liang Zhu. It has been told to me many times, and every time I hear it I want to cry. I believe that this story, like Romeo and Juliet, shows us that love between two persons can be affected by social conditions. None of us loves in a vacuum. Today, especially, love becomes a complex subject because of the many complexities of our society.

As you say, the expression of love between two persons is more open in China than it used to be. This is a good example of how romantic relationships take place within a culture and are affected by the history and traditions of the culture. You ask a very interesting and important question: With more freedom in choosing mates, why is the divorce rate growing? There is no easy answer to this question, and no experts on the subject. If you were to ask several professionals this question, you probably would get several different answers.

My own feeling is that romantic love and marriage are not the same. A romantic loving relationship is not necessarily a loving marriage. Romance may be based on physical attractions. We may be attracted to another person by their appearance, by the car they drive, by the gifts they give us, by their status in the community, or by many other qualities. After marriage, some of these qualities become less important. Some are replaced by problems that arise after the wedding.

Marriage is a complex affair in every culture and especially complex in industrial societies where there is more social intercourse between persons. Marriage also involves other persons who were not part of the romantic scene. Marriage places values on parental relations, on child rearing, on financial decisions, on long term ambitions, and on a host of other matters that probably were not considered during the romantic courtship. Marriage also places a couple into a society which has its own traditions and expectations.

It is also true that we change as we grow older. Our outlook on life and on activities changes. We grow at different rates. Our interests change. Our physical and emotional needs become different. Our level of communication is not the same as it was during our courtship period. In many couples, the adjustment to changing conditions is not the same.

Perhaps another reason for the growing divorce rate is that under the older method of choosing mates, it was the parents who made the selection. Under that system, a couple would be more hesitant to divorce because a divorce would question the judgment of the parents who put the marriage together.

Best wishes for success in life, in love, and in marriage, Bob

▲

Dear Bob,

I am a college student. Recently, I discovered that I am in love with a girl who is very pretty. We are good friends. She is extroverted and lively. I love her very much, but I don't have the courage to tell her because I am afraid that I might enrage her and ruin the friendship. I am really in deep misery.

What should I do, Bob? Can you help me?

Your loyal reader, Miserable (Shanghai)

▲

Dear Miserable,

Thank you for your letter. I do not consider myself an expert on giving love advice. This is such a personal matter and a very complex subject. It involves personal emotions, culture, social considerations, personalities, temperaments, and a host of other elements.

Having cleared all these generalities, let's get to the heart of your question and begin with a bit of analysis. The relevant facts seem to be the following: You are in love with a girl. You are afraid to tell her this because it might ruin your friendship with her.

If I were you under these circumstances, I would meet with her, perhaps over an ice cream soda or whatever dessert she prefers. Remember that eye contact is most important. Look at her softly but directly into her eyes. As a first step, you might come directly to the point by asking her, "If I were to tell you that I love you, how would you react?" This should not make her angry because you are merely asking, "If . . ." If you listen carefully to her reply, you will get a sense of what to say next.

Miserable, if you try this, or some other approach, please let me know the result. It might be helpful to me in case I have the same problem as you have now. This is a crazy world, and someday, if you are successful, I might need to ask your opinion.

Good luck, and if the girl is pretty and smart, she will tell you that she has been waiting for you to ask her this. Let me know.

With warm regards and best wishes, Bob

P.S. If your approach is not successful, it is still better than doing nothing. The sooner you find out how this girl views you, the better for you. It is important that you get on with your life and get this worry behind you.

▲

Dear Bob,

Thank you for your advice. I still do not have the courage to do it. Let me think about it. I will tell you right after I have done it.

Goodbye! Miserable (Shanghai)

▲

Dear Miserable,

Thank you for asking me to help you to find favor with the girl of your dreams. As you point out, there are large cultural differences between the Chinese and the American societies. These differences are especially apparent in male-female relationships during school years. Both are changing rapidly. All I can do is to wish you success. From a distance, it seems that your success will depend on how bold you can be, and how confident you can be in your approach to her.

Just keep telling yourself how good and beautiful you are, and how fortunate she will be if she spends time with you.

I hope the results of your silent courtship are successful. And remember that timing is important. You need to select the best time and the best place to speak with her.

Respectfully yours, Bob

▲

Dear Bob,

The girl of my dreams came to borrow my badminton racket, but I couldn't find it. I borrowed one and sent it to her in person. Why did she come to me for the racket? I do not know. Could you help me, Bob? When she sees me alone, she talks to me warmly; when she sees me with others nearby, she never talks to me. Why does she do this? Bob, have you had a similar experience? Thank you for giving me so much help. I am very introverted.

Thank you! Miserable (Shanghai)

▲

Dear Miserable,

I am fascinated by your attempts to woo your "dream girl." This is the stuff that movies, plays, and novels are made of. Abelard and Romeo and now Miserable—a good combination.

Asking to borrow your badminton racket seems like a good sign. It shows that she wants to share one of your possessions with you. It will be a better sign if she returns it to you without damage.

As we agreed before, love is a mysterious matter, and it is the mystery that gives it charm. Sorry that it is giving you so much anxiety. Have you thought of inviting this girl to play badminton? I have developed good relationships with persons over the ping pong table. Maybe you can do this while playing badminton?

Please don't give up hope too easily or too quickly. Many girls like the shy boys best. I hope that she does. Maybe I will be congratulating you on your wedding some day. What do you think?

With best wishes, Bob

▲

Dear Bob,

I think you are right. If I do not express myself, how will the girl know I love her? I am ready to ask her, "If I said 'I love you,' how would you react?" But if she says, "I do not love you," or "I have a boyfriend already," what should I do next?

I expect your reply. Thank you, Bob.

Miserable (Shanghai)

▲

Dear Miserable,

You seem to be making progress, especially when you write that you feel it is necessary to express yourself.

If you are hesitant to speak directly to her, you might want to consider sending her a note which would say something like this: "I am very fond of you, but I do not know your feelings toward me. I am shy about asking you this in person, but it is important for me to know. Please tell me if you are as fond of me as I am fond of you."

You would have to put this in your best Chinese and hope for a favorable reply. In this way, you might know her feelings. If they are favorable, great; I might look forward to a wedding announcement sometime in the future. If they are not favorable, it is better that you find out now so you can get on with your life and perhaps meet other young women who will be more receptive to your charms. This also might result in a wedding announcement, even though it is to a different young woman.

Sorry I can't suggest the proper Chinese words. Maybe Mahya could be of help to you on this. She is my Dearest editor and has supreme judgment.

Keep trying. I am waiting for the results. Bob

▲

Dear Bob,

A few days ago, I invited the girl to a place. She turned me down, but she is still nice to me. What should I do? Does she know that I love her? I think she should know because she has a higher IQ than many others.

Miserable (Shanghai)

▲

Dear Miserable,

If you believe that you can make your dream girl happy, you probably have the same IQ she has. Please use your IQ and study (not just read) all of Bob's letters to you. I am sure that you will be able to figure out a way to get the girl and/or to get out of the misery.

My best wishes for a happy life, Mahya

Study Abroad

Dear Bob,

I have been confused these days.

I am sixteen years old. My friends tell me that this is the best time to study abroad and that it is not difficult for teenagers to get used to another culture. They emphasize that the earlier one goes abroad, the easier it is to become accustomed to a foreign country. They say that in America and England, the students are taught in a more creative way than in China.

I cannot make a decision. I would like to go abroad to get a better education. I do not know if I can manage everything by myself. Some students who went abroad failed and were sent back.

I am not eager to just follow others, but I do not want to lose any chances. Would you please give me some suggestions? Thank you very much.

With my best wishes, Nina (Beijing)

Dear Nina,

Your letter raises an interesting question: Is it better for a Chinese student to go abroad for study or to stay in China?

There are so many considerations which must be weighed in making such a decision. These include the level of experience and sophistication of the student, the added financial expense, the separation from family and friends, the risks of being in a strange culture, the impact on career choices, and many more.

I have heard that American education is more creative than Chinese education. I am unable to judge this because I am not familiar with the Chinese system. I know that both systems are turning out superior graduates.

There are advantages of becoming familiar with different educational and cultural environments and meeting students with a variety of backgrounds and experiences. Travel can offer many opportunities to broaden one's perspective, but this depends upon the student. I have known some students who have flourished in American universities, and there are others who are not comfortable living and studying in a foreign society.

Nina, after weighing all the advantages and disadvantages, there is always the luck element. It is not easy to anticipate some of the conditions that one may find including the choice of a roommate, adjustment to different weather patterns, level of faculty involvement, and social activities. My own feeling is that travel and study in a foreign country favor the more mature student, especially the student who is adventuresome (both physically and mentally) and who is emotionally able to adjust to change. For this reason, I would prefer to take graduate studies abroad rather than undergraduate studies.

Because I do not know you, I am unable to help in your decision. My only advice is to give this very careful consideration because it is a big decision and one which will have an impact on your entire future. You might be wise to consult with your family, and to seek the experiences of friends who might have gone abroad for their education.

Best wishes for a bright future (whether it is in China or abroad), Bob

Dear Mahya,

Please give my thanks and best wishes to Bob. I am not confused anymore. I am sure about what I should do.

Best wishes, Nina (Beijing)

Agape

Dear Bob,

I cannot agree more with the idea that children never outgrow their need to be loved. I think that love for children can be divided into two parts. One is "material love" and the other is "spiritual love." Nowadays, children are not short on "material love" but "spiritual love." Parents and the whole society should pay more attention to giving their children the real love, "spiritual love."

Best regards, Ge Pei (Nanjing, Jiangsu)

▲

Dear Pei,

I thank you for the comments you sent to me about children needing to be loved. Even though we are far apart (China and America), we are very close in our feelings about children. In our relationship to children, sometimes our expectations get in the way of our love.

Your letter brings back memories of a conversation I overheard between two children. One child said, "I got an 'A'." The second child replied, "That is too bad." The first child said, "What did you get?" "I got a 'C'." "Why is that better than an 'A'?" the first child asked. "Because life is easier when everyone has lower expectations of you."

Maybe there is a lesson here for all of us, whether we are in China or in America.

Respectfully yours, Bob

Humor

Hi, Dr. Robert S. Herman,

I am one of your readers from China. I like learning English, and I like your works very much, especially "Animals."

"Humor is truly the shortest distance between people," is so wise. I think the joke about the pig and the cow is full of wit. I have read the story about the duck and the pharmacist in Chinese. Now I got to read the English edition, and it's so humorous.

In the article, you said you had worked in more than a dozen different countries. I envy you so much. I have never gone to a foreign country, so I hope I can go abroad one day.

Best regards!

Your, Wu Pengfei (Wendeng, Shandong)

▲

Dear Pengfei,

I am pleased that you enjoy humor and that you share this with me. You envy persons who have "gone to foreign countries." I understand this. Travel sometimes gives a person a broader perspective and new experiences.

However, it is also true that there are other ways of traveling. We do not have to go to foreign countries. We can "travel" by learning, by reading, and by developing our own mental powers—without ever leaving home. I believe that this is what you are doing. I have learned more in my own library than I have in traveling to distant places.

I hope that you find opportunities to travel to other countries, but always remember that you are "traveling" every day with your own mind and your own imagination.

With good wishes, Bob

Hello, Bob,

Nice meeting you on the web. I'm so excited that you wrote a letter to me. It's so important to me, a Chinese boy who is learning English. What you said in the letter is so useful, and I'm so appreciative. Thanks!

Best regards! Yours, Wu Pengfei (Wendeng, Shandong)

Peace

Hi, Bob,

You are a gorgeous guy who was born to write fascinating stories and captivating poems. I was deeply impressed by your poem, "Nothings." It's my favorite.

And now I would be honored and very enthralled if I could have a chance to share our thoughts. I am sending a paper to you and am longing for your comments on it.

Peace and Development (To Weed and Sow)

Good afternoon, friends!

I am very happy to join you today in sharing our thoughts on this subject of "Peace and Development" that we recognize as an enormous need in our world.

A year ago, we were shocked by the horror of September 11, and, soon after, the strife caused by the tension between India and Pakistan. Around the world, tragedies continue to occur, in the theatre in Moscow and in the restaurant in Bali.

Today, even as we speak, a girl from a penniless family in Afghanistan could be forced to make a living by prostitution, or a boy in Palestine could be training to be a suicide bomber for the vengeance of his suicidal father.

So we ask, why do these things have to happen? And what is the root of all these grievous stories? My answer would be that the disease leading to those bloody wars and endless suffering are the seeds of prejudice, egoism, and fear.

When the seeds of prejudice spread, some believe that their people are superior to other people, their culture is better than other cultures, and their way is the only and correct way. Hence, only they have the right to possess truth and fortune. Nazism arose.

When the seeds of egoism spread, some would only like to live in a universe of their own making and seek their power and pleasure by striking dread into the hearts and minds of others who do share their value system. And terrorism arose.

When the seeds of fear spread, some tend to strike them out by force, which usually increases the fear, especially for people caught up in a retaliation cycle, as is present in Israel and formerly in Ireland. Both sides continually live in fear, and the cry of moaning and weeping persists.

Ladies and gentlemen, to safeguard world peace and promote common development, we must weed the seeds of prejudice, egoism, and fear out of our lives, and, at the same time, plant the seeds of friendship, dedication, and gratitude.

If the seeds of friendship were sown—and that friendship would not judge or compel other nations, but learn about and celebrate their unique qualities—we would be less inclined, and have less reason, to shoot each other. Instead, we would be more likely to help and support each other, hand in hand.

If the seeds of dedication were sown, we would shift our attention from busily serving our greed and vanity to the primary concern of all humankind—peace, food, security, economic development, and the environment.

If the seeds of gratitude were sown, gratitude for living on this beautiful planet, we would combine all nations' brainpower and do everything we could to perpetuate "Peace and Development" year by year, generation by generation, and century by century.

This task is particularly urgent with the acceleration of scientific and technological progress. Professionals tell us that as the Net evolves, all machines and people will become nodes on a network, and one computer will be able to tap the power of all. Consequently, as we can see, the world will be much, much more dangerous if we fail to achieve our task.

My friends, to avoid this conceivable chaos and destruction, we must take action and take it now. I hereby make an emphatic call on each of us to plant these seeds of friendship, dedication, and gratitude in his own heart and soul, as we want to plant them throughout the world. A world we live in, a world that is peaceful, pleasant, modern, and healthily developed.

Thank you very much!

Peter Cheng (Shanghai)

▲

Dear Peter,

Thank you for sharing your thoughts with me. I am impressed by what you wrote. Your insights into our world condition are true and powerful. I hope they will be read by more people. Yes, as you say, prejudice, egoism, and fear are some of the reasons for the pathetic state of our planet. I would add greed, pride, and envy.

When we look at the resources we inherited with this beautiful planet, the pure air and water, the fertile soil, and the magnificent human and animal capabilities, it is a wonder why present living conditions are so tragically poor for so many of our earth citizens.

We have learned to till the soil, yet there is starvation and hunger for so many. We have achieved technical excellence in communication, yet we use it to threaten our neighbors. We have developed air conditioning and central heating, yet so many are dying of heat or cold. We have discovered new medical treatments for so many illnesses, yet millions are dying for lack of treatment. Billions of people face food and water shortages because of the environmental devastation. The list goes on and on!

We are attacking this planet as if it were an enemy instead of our home. We are cheating not only ourselves but our children. If we continue on our present path, the planet they inherit will be filled with wars, with pollution, with strife, and with fear. What a shame! Our planetary society is so fragile that what occurs in one part can damage other parts.

I believe that one of the sources of all this tragedy is the lust for power and for money. This is unfortunate. Maybe it is the lack of love that causes the lust for power. It is hard for me to understand why persons need to build stockpiles of money and accumulate such an abundance of material possessions when their tenure on this earth is so temporary.

Your thoughts stimulated me to respond and I find myself agreeing with much of what you wrote. Please continue to write.

With warm regards and best wishes, Bob

▲

Hi, Bob!

My friend, it was a great joy to receive your letter. I have a gut feeling that we two could be very good friends.

I have read your letter word for word, and I do agree with what you said.

A very good friend of mine told me that in northwestern Montana, there is a tree with pinecones that do not release its seeds until a fire occurs. Fires can sometimes provide fertile ground, releasing good seeds and growing strong trees for the future.

I like the saying that to have peace in the world, we have to have peace in our own homes and hearts. That is a good place to begin. Next, we can see how we are contributing to our own homes and nations. Because of e-mail, we easily communicate with people across the nation and the world. Bridges are being built. Oh, how I would love to be able to live in another culture for semester or a year! I strongly believe that the foreigner and all who interact with him or her are changed forever. There is so much to value in other cultures, and anything that is lost is lost to the whole world.

Sincerely yours, Peter Cheng (Shanghai)

Dear Peter,

Thank you for calling me your friend. This is a compliment for me. Your poem, "An Evening Walk" [included in a prior letter to Bob], is a delight to read. Of course, I do not know the lady it was written to, but I hope that it will evoke a very cordial response. She should be impressed by the depth of your feelings and your ability to put these into such a beautiful poem.

Your words flow like honey, and I especially like the line, "Turn the earth as a magic mirror." I hope you will continue to write poems. The February issue of *Overseas English* is scheduled to publish a poem that I wrote to my wife to celebrate our 60th wedding anniversary. You will see that I share your interest in writing "love poems."

I share your sentiments about peace and suffering. In this world, we have too much suffering and too little peace. This will be a better world when more persons share feelings like yours. We must find ways to make the power of love more important and more universal than the love of power.

Respectfully yours, Bob

▲

Hi, Bob,

This is Peter! Remember?

I have been reading and enjoying your articles and poems. I am happy that you are so popular in China. I think it's the love and concern you hold for this world that we Chinese people admire. I hope you have some time to look through Chinese ancient poems and stories. I bet there are a lot that can inspire you in some way.

As you know, my major is Finance, and I know how to train myself to be a great financier, like Andre Meyer. All the people around me think that this is the best career for me.

Mama would spend three hours bargaining or walk six miles just to save one yuan. Sometimes I have a guilty conscience if I buy things or want nice clothes, and I know exactly how being rich is going to change things. At the same time, I know what I want, what I like, and what kind of life I am looking for. You see, I am a crazy romantic person.

Sincerely yours, Peter (Shanghai)

▲

Dear Peter,

It was a pleasure to receive your letter. I like the way you write English, and I like your attitude toward life. Yes, I do admire ancient Chinese poems and stories. There is so much wisdom in China, old and new. In fact, there is much wisdom all over the world, and I am sorry that we do not act upon it. You have given me a good idea for writing a column on this topic.

Your choice of Finance as a major sounds like a good one, and I think you will be successful in the world of finance. It can be very competitive and challenging. You say that you are "a crazy romantic person." This may be good if you can find romance in finance.

If you keep studying and keep your goals high, I know that you are going to have a very successful future. Maybe someday you will become a director of the Bank of China. If you do, maybe I will try to borrow one yuan from you.

With best wishes and warm regards, Bob

Competition

Bob,

I am sure you have already found that there are a lot of people here in China. Have you noticed what it means for us, as students? The competition is maddening.

I am worried. People ask me, "After you put yourself through college, what are you planning to do? Will you pursue your studies to be a postgraduate or hunt for a good job?"

I see a lot of people, including myself, struggling to find themselves. I am dying to hear your advice on this topic to people of my age.

Respectfully yours, Peter Cheng (Shanghai)

▲

Dear Peter,

It is sad to learn that "competition is maddening" among young persons in China. This is also true in other countries. I have found that competition may bring out the best in products, but the worst in people. This can also be reversed because there are times when competition brings us shabby products. It can also have a wholesome effect of people. It all depends on the specific situation.

We are all struggling to find ourselves. Life is a constant search. It only ends when we end. I have thought that an appropriate notation on gravestones might be "I have arrived." Life is a journey, and the only time we arrive is when we are dead.

I enjoy reading all your insights. Knowing ourselves is most important. This may be the most important search we all have—the search into ourselves. I hope that when someone knocks on my head, they will not find it empty!

Your advice about taking action is also on target. The great goal in life must be more than the accumulation of knowledge. It must be to use the knowledge we have accumulated, and to use it for some noble purpose.

Peter, keep thinking and keep writing. You have much to say, and you say it very well.

With best wishes, Bob

War

Bob,

My friend, war began. I feel sorry for this. I feel sorry that, inevitably, someone will be dead, someone will lose his parents, and someone will lose his sons.

Is it really inevitable? I doubt it. One of my American friends said, "War does not create peace. Ghandi knew that, and Martin Luther King, and Jesus and, no doubt, Buddha."

I hear children moaning at an Iraqi hospital. Children do not deserve this kind of trauma, nor are these the images we would want them to carry into their adulthood. I hear Iraq's museum has been destroyed. Anything that is lost is lost to the whole world. I hear parents on both sides are praying for their children.

There must be some other way. We should stop the war. Then, perhaps, like the phoenix, we can rise from the ashes and build a better world that embraces the whole human family and celebrates what is unique in each of us.

What do you think, Bob?

Always yours, Peter Cheng (Shanghai)

▲

Dear Peter,

Thank you again for writing to Mahya and me. We appreciate the time and effort you are devoting to the important subject of war and peace. Maybe we should turn this phrase around and call it peace and war! This would show our priorities better.

We seem to agree on the need to obliterate wars. Fortunately most people will agree with this need. It is a basic requirement for the survival of this planet, yet wars continue. This is such a paradox. We speak peace and we wage war.

In order to eliminate wars, we must eliminate the causes of wars. Please do not give up your search for peace.

With best wishes, Bob

▲

Hello, Bob! Hello, Mahya!

I got goosebumps when I bought the magazine today. My letters are printed in my favorite magazine. I must be envied.

Well, frankly, these days all my friends and I have shifted our attention from job-seeking to the war in Iraq, so I am more concerned with Bob's reply to my latest letter. I hope our dialogue will continue.

I have sent the magazine to my Mom. I am sure she will be happy to see her son's words in print, though she can't read English. I have never done anything great like this. Mom will be thrilled. It's a great honor to any mom. Thank you.

Best wishes, Peter Cheng (Shanghai)

Moonstruck

Dear Sir,

I am one of your loyal readers. I would like to express my feelings about the topic of last month's column, "Love."

Love is a subtle thing. It is abstract. What is its appearance? How and when did it come into being? We do not have the answers. But sometimes, love turns out to be inevitable. For everyone lives on earth; it is inevitable that we will relate to others. Love is omnipresent.

Love is letting the other person be who he is. If you love him, give him freedom. Your lover is not your ideal model. It is stupid to attempt to change someone based on your own wants. If you have a crush on someone, maybe it is his differences that attract you. If you love him, let him keep his own temperament. Love is momentum and an obstacle. Every coin has two sides.

Being loved, I feel the value of my existence. Maybe I am exaggerating, but it is my true feeling.

Sir, this is my first letter to you. Can you give me some advice?

Your sincerely, Polaris

▲

Dear Polaris,

It is a pleasure to know that you read my article on "Love." I tried to express some of my feelings on this elusive subject. Your response is excellent.

You say that love is subtle. It sure is. It is also mysterious. Love and money are our two greatest sources of pleasure and our two greatest sources of anxiety at the same time.

I am interested in your saying that love is "inevitable." This makes me think. I hope that it is inevitable, and, in the long run, it must be inevitable if this planet is to survive. In terms of our behavior and our relationships, love seems to be in competition with other emotions such as fear and hate and envy and pride and greed, to mention only a few.

I hope, as you do, that love will triumph over all these rivals. Only time will tell us if this will happen. This fierce struggle is taking place within each of us. It is also taking place everywhere else in the world. Love will be victorious if you and I and millions of others are determined to make it triumph.

My best wishes to you, Bob

▲

Dear Bob,

Thanks for your advice. I'm feeling better now.

Sometimes love is transient. I get such feeling from the story of my roommate. She was chased by a man. When they were together, something happened. Then she went steady with him. She doesn't know why she made such a decision. Maybe it's unreasonable. Maybe it was an impulse. Who cares? It's exhausting to live so cautiously all the time.

Thanks again, Bob and Mahya, for your encouragement. Yours truly, Polaris

▲

Dear Polaris,

I am happy that my words have made you feel better. Mahya and I agree that being loved and being able to love are two of the greatest gifts that we humans have been given. Your roommate will have to work out her own problems. I don't know of any prescription for loving that can be applied to everyone—or to anyone.

Each of us has a distinct personality and temperament. Each of us is an exception. Each of us must learn what we can love, how we can love, and what we expect from love. And all of this usually changes as we grow and mature.

My best wishes for your roommate. Respectfully yours, Bob

Speaking English

Dear Bob,

I read most of your articles in *English Salon*, and, to tell the truth, I contemplate much and achieve much every time after reading your articles.

English is my major. I have spent much time practicing speaking, but I have made little progress. I was told that my oral English is unpleasant to listen to. This distresses me very much. Please tell me how to speak English fluently.

Your devoted reader, Rain (Chongqing)

▲

Dear Rain,

Thank you for writing to Bob. I am glad that you have pored over Bob's articles. Yes, many readers tell me that Bob's column has changed their perspectives and even their personal lives.

Bob isn't available right now, but I am happy to share my thoughts with you.

The comment, "unpleasant," regardless of whom it is from, is not fair to you. Even Americans speak in different tones and manners, just like the different dialects we speak in China.

Our mother tongue plays an important role in all language learning. I was born in China and have lived in the U.S. for over 10 years. Once I open my mouth, people can tell that I am a foreigner and that English is my second language. This is fine with me, because the intention of learning a language is to communicate with others. Of course, it would be a gift if we could sound like TV anchors.

Practice makes you perfect. There is no better way than to practice, which you are doing now. It will take time to become a fluent speaker, especially in terms of learning a foreign language when we are no longer children. If you see yourself as helpless, you act helpless. See yourself as strong; then you will become strong.

Best wishes, Mahya

▲

Dear Rain,

Thank you for writing to me. I just read the response that my colleague and editor, Mahya, wrote to you. Her advice is splendid, and there is nothing that I could add. Mahya has learned to speak and write in English with remarkable fluency. Please heed her advice carefully.

With warm regards, Bob

Brave New You

Dear Bob,

Thank you for replying! I'm very glad to receive your letter. Thanks to the editor, she is very responsible indeed. I will continue being your devoted reader.

I want to ask a popular question. How can I build up confidence as an ordinary girl? Thanks for sharing your thoughts with me!

Rain (Chongqing)

▲

Dear Rain,

Thank you for your letter and your question about achieving "confidence" in ourselves. This is one of the most common questions that Chinese readers have asked me. There is no easy answer. Each of us has a distinct personality and temperament. Every one of us needs to find ways to protect our ego. We live in complicated social environments where our ego can be in competition with the ego needs of other persons.

For many persons, confidence comes with experience. It can come with success. It usually depends upon our relationship with others. When we are successful in our relationships and in our careers, we usually feel better about ourselves. One answer to your question would be to spend your time and energy building better relationships with your friends and family and colleagues. If you are successful in finding affection and love and support in these relationships, you should feel better about yourself.

I have found that persons who seem to have the most confidence in themselves are persons who view their world positively rather than negatively. We seem to be attracted to persons who are cheerful and hopeful. A smile is still the best way to improve your appearance, in spite of the advice given to us in advertisements for cosmetics.

Confidence can come from within us as well as from our relationships with others. This can be a matter of practice. If we can constantly remind ourselves that we are beautiful works of art, that we are here on earth to serve others, that we can absorb stress, and that we can adapt to changes, then we should develop a strong sense of our self esteem which is another way of saying our self confidence.

Try to remind yourself that everyone you meet is having the same problem of finding self esteem. You are not alone in asking this question. Maybe if you can find ways to help others find more self confidence in themselves, yours will improve in the process?

It has been interesting for me to write these words to you. I share your concern for achieving self esteem. It is letters like yours and the friendships that have come to me from our Chinese readers that have helped me to maintain confidence in myself. For this I am eternally grateful to all of you.

With best wishes and warm regards, Bob

Dear Bob,

Thank you for replying! Your response is always prompt. I am very happy after reading your letter. I hope I can keep in touch with you by e-mail. I need a great guide like you!

Best wishes.

Your Chinese friend, Rain (Chongqing)

▲

Dear Bob,

I just know that you are over 80 years old! I was surprised and moved very much! I think I will be like you when I'm old. You are such a great man who is worthy of our Chinese respect.

I want to tell you something about one of my friend. In my eyes, she is very beautiful and cute. Many of our friends, boys and girls, are fond of her, and sometimes I almost envy her. But she always tells me that she is not happy and she often feels nervous in public. She always thinks that others look at her. I'm puzzled, and I turn to you for help. What can she do and what can I do to help her as her friend?

Best Wishes, Rain (Chongqing)

▲

Dear Rain,

Your letter sounds more "upbeat" (there is a new word for you) than your last one. I am sorry that your friend is not happy, and that she feels nervous in public. She obviously needs to get more confidence in herself.

The best advice I can give you for her is to ask her to read the letter I sent to you. (If you can read that sentence, you are very proficient in English!) Do you remember that I told you all I know about trying to gain confidence? Try it on her and let's see if it has any effect.

From what you wrote, your friend is young, beautiful, and popular with both boys and girls. These are fine qualities, and I hope she will be able to build upon them.

With best wishes for her, and warm regards to you, Bob

▲

Dear Rain,

Thank you for writing to Bob and helping your friend as well. You are very kind.

Do you know that your happiness and kindness are contagious? Please try to spend more time with your troubled friend and share Bob's columns with her. Bob and I will be happy to hear good news from you soon.

Best regards, Mahya

Troubles

Dear Bob,

I was very glad to read your article in *English Salon*. It has made a deep impression on me. I admire your profound knowledge and am eager to write to you. I'd like to tell you about some of my troubles, and I want to ask you for advice.

I'm now a freshman at a university in eastern China. I'm an ordinary girl. I'm not a beauty, so I want to be good at my studies. I study very hard. However, as the final scores came out, I wasn't at the top. I might not be able to get a scholarship. I feel rather miserable.

My parents are farmers. They work hard for my tuition in spite of their old age, and they have high hopes for me. I feel great pressure. Would you tell me what to do?

Rebecah

Dear Rebecah,

Congratulations on being a freshman at a university. That is an accomplishment to be proud of. I know how severe the competition is in China for university acceptance. I hope you do not let yourself become discouraged over the scholarship. You are studying hard and that is all that you can do. Not everyone can be first in the class.

I am sure that your parents are proud of you and that they have worked hard for your tuition. This should be an incentive for you to attend to your studies and to think about what you intend to do with your life after you complete your university education. Please try to think about all that you have achieved so far in your young life. I am sure that there are millions of young Chinese who would like to be where you are.

My experience has made me believe that a positive attitude toward myself and my life is much more rewarding than having a negative attitude. You may not reach every goal that you are setting for yourself. I never reached all of mine. No one does. We have to build on our experience and look ahead eagerly to what we can do next.

From your letter, I know that you have achieved much already. If you can keep a positive attitude, and perhaps a sense of humor about yourself, I feel that you will be very successful in life.

Please tell your parents that I have faith in you. I know they will agree with me.

With best wishes, Bob

▲

Dear Bob,

Thank you very much. My thoughts have changed a lot since I read your letter. I'm so glad to tell you that I just got a job as an English teacher. I got a high score on the national examination last year. I can get some money from this, which will also reduce my parents' burden. I feel very happy.

In your passage, you say that you have never been to China. What a pity! You are welcome to China, and also to my hometown. I'd be very glad to be your guide.

Yours, Rebecah

Aging

Dear Bob,

I'm a faithful and enthusiastic reader of *Overseas English*. Your articles have furthered my interest in it. Now, reading the magazine is part of my monthly routine! Thanks, Bob.

I learned that you are over eighty years old. I'm really shocked. From your positive attitude towards life and the picture of you above each of your articles, I was sure that you were middle-aged. It led me into deep contemplation.

I'm a sophomore at Jilin University. Most of the people my age believe that the elderly are useless and their experience is out-of-date. That is not how I see it. In my opinion, our youth should care much more about the elderly. Sympathy is not necessary. Material offerings are not enough. Appreciation of their experience and wisdom is what is needed. Being old is a part of life. Without it, life would not be a harmonious whole.

I often imagine my spouse and me sitting in the sunset with our white hair. It's so quiet, peaceful, and charming. None of my friends can understand me. It would be great if you could share your view with us about this problem. I really appreciate your consideration and time.

By the way, Merry Christmas!

Yours, Rebecca (Changchun, Jilin)

▲

Dear Rebecca,

You and I share a common interest in the aging process. I appreciate your comments on this important subject.

I agree with your opinions about old age, and I have the experience to prove that you are correct. It is sad to hear that many young persons in China view the experience of the elderly as "out-of-date," according to your letter. When I was teaching, I would tell my students to be careful what they say about older persons, because they may live to regret it.

Aging is a part of life, and it can be an exciting and rewarding part. It has been said that aging is like climbing a mountain; the higher you get, the more tired and breathless you become, but the view becomes much more extensive. I find that instead of looking back to how beautiful we looked or how we excelled in athletics, it is better to look ahead to see what still needs to be done. Sure, we do experience some physical decline, but we make up for this with greater psychological growth.

Chronological age can also be confusing. I have some friends who were 40 when they were born. And I feel that I was older 50 years ago than I am now. Does this make sense to you?

Of course each of us has our distinct personality and temperament. We each have our own view of life, and each of us must decide what we expect from it, and, I hope, what we hope to give to it. Old age can be a time of serenity and also a time of adventure. It can be a time for reflection and a time for involvement.

As we grow older, I believe that time becomes more and more important to us. Time becomes a matter of fascination, and sometimes a matter of worry.

Thank you for sharing your thoughts with me. I value them. And "Rebecca" is one of my favorite names. It was my grandmother's name.

With warm regards and best wishes, Bob

Modern Society

Dear Bob,

I am a student at Jiangxi University, but I am different from others. I am a polio patient. My parents and my friends love me very much. However, I still feel helpless in our modern society.

How can I confront the future, which is difficult for disabled people? I am very interested in your column, and hope you can give me some advice.

Respectfully yours, River (Nanchang, Jiangxi)

▲

Dear River,

Being a student at Jiangxi University tells me that you have accomplished much in spite of a handicap. Congratulations on reaching the university level. You have achieved much already.

Being a polio patient does present added problems for you. I can understand this. But it also presents you with wonderful opportunities. I have found that among my friends, the most successful ones are those who have had to overcome handicaps. These handicaps have provided them with added strength of purpose and determination.

We often say that the brook would stop singing if we removed the rocks. Obstacles can be turned into advantages. A smooth life can be less productive than a life which has had obstacles to overcome.

Each of us has a mental and an emotional side in addition to a physical side. My experience is that we are admired much more for our mental and emotional achievements than we are for our physical ones—unless we happen to be professional athletes. Even athletes need to depend on their mental and emotional strengths in order to be successful.

River, of course you did not choose to have polio. I understand that it does limit you in some ways. But please try to use your infirmity to give you more strength and more purpose in life. You do have one big advantage. Having a handicap makes you more sensitive to those who are less fortunate than others. This sensitivity is needed in the world, and may give you the incentive to help those who are less privileged.

I have several friends who have had polio in their youth. All of these persons have led very full lives and have gotten much satisfaction by having overcome their initial handicap. I believe that you will too.

Please try to avoid the trap of feeling sorry for yourself. Instead, use your infirmity as a basis for adding love and purpose to others in this world who can profit from your insights and sensitivity.

With warm regards and best wishes, Bob

▲

Dear Bob,

Thank you very much for writing such a long letter to me. What you wrote encouraged me and moved me. Having a handicap affects every aspect of one's life. Many of the difficulties of daily living are hard to express in a letter and hard to overcome. Normal persons might never imagine the life we endure.

I write this letter to you with the hope that more and more people can understand and respect us. I am encouraged when you tell me that we can achieve more because we suffer more.

I am only a common college student. I enjoy my studies, and my classmates treat me very well. I hope everyone can be happy.

With warm regards and best wishes, River
(Nanchang, Jiangxi)

▲

Dear River,

I am grateful for your second letter. I admire your outlook on life in spite of your handicap. Of course, this handicap affects every part of your life. It is good that you can write about it to me. It is also good that you are able to make friends with your classmates.

It is easy to "give in" to a handicap. I am proud of you for not doing this. There is along life ahead of you, and I sense that it will be a successful life for you **because** of your physical handicap, and not **in spite of it**!

I just read my previous letter to you. To know my feelings about you, I suggest that you read my letter again. I wish only to remind you that Franklin Roosevelt also suffered from polio, and he became President of the United States. This should provide you with great motivation and much encouragement.

With best wishes, Bob

Journey Through Life

Dear Dr. Herman,

I just read your column, "Adventures of the Mind," in *Overseas English*. You told us that a college education is important in one's life. Yes, I think so too. I found that both my view of the world and my attitude towards life, as well as my character, have changed due to my education at a university. My college experience was good preparation for my lifelong trip.

Now, however, all has changed again. I have graduated from a normal university and am teaching at a school at present. Life is boring for me now. The reality is very different from what I had imagined at the university. At that time, I thought I would work hard and devote myself to teaching. I worked hard in the first year and tried my best to help my students. Later, I found that many of my colleagues were very idle, and students were absent-minded in class. It has been a big disappointment for me. Sometimes I feel the need to change my job, but I fear that every kind of work has its own difficulty. I wonder what I should do. Can you help me?

Yours, Salin (Ningbo, Zhejiang)

Dear Salin,

Our journey through life can be cluttered with disappointments like the ones you describe. It is often necessary to change our route, and even to question our destination.

However, your desire to teach is so commendable, and our need for good teachers (both in America and in China) is very great. Please do not give up too soon or too easily. You might consider changing the location of your teaching, finding different students who will learn from you, or seeking new methods of making your knowledge and experience available to your students.

If every attempt fails, a change in your career is always a possibility. I have had many career changes in my life, and I have learned much from every one.

I know that you will succeed in whatever career you finally decide upon.

My best wishes, Bob

Valentine's Day

Dear Bob,

In *Overseas English*, I like your column best. Today, I was deeply impressed by your poem to your wife in your column titled "Love." It touched me so much that I couldn't help writing this letter to you.

You are right that Valentine's Day is celebrated in China every year. I think this is because love exists everywhere and belongs to everyone. You say love is letting another person be who he or she is. I cannot really understand love because I have never really experienced any romantic love. However, I agree that "the most important thing in life is to love someone. The second most important thing in life is to have someone love you. The third most important thing is to have the first two happen at the same time." It is so difficult to have the third thing happen.

Although I am only 25, I have not met anyone whom I love. I will not love someone when I don't know whether he loves me or not. Of course, I know it is not possible to love without giving, but I am afraid of being hurt.

Maybe I am too young to understand love; maybe I have a lack of self-confidence.

I like your article. Thank you very much. Your words have taught me much.

With best wishes, Salin (Ningbo, Zhejiang)

▲

Dear Salin,

I am pleased that you were impressed by my poem. Love is a complex emotion and is different for every one of us. I can understand your fear of being hurt by loving. This can happen. It is usually the result of a lack of self-confidence. We must assume that confidence will come with experience. I hope that all your future experiences with love will be happy ones.

With best wishes, Bob

Literature

Dear Bob,

I looked through *English Salon* and was very excited to find your column. As a college student majoring in English, I have no problem understanding you.

I have learned English for almost eight years. It is not hard for me to communicate with foreigners. However, when I read novels written by Dickens or Rip Van Winkle written by Washington Irving, I get lost.

The more barriers I meet, the less confident I become. I forced myself to read something more challenging, and I decided to scan the twenty-six essays from a book named Great American Short Stories during winter break.

What is your opinion? I am looking forward to your e-mail.

Sincerely, Sema (Beijing)

Dear Sema,

I am impressed at the excellence of your English. You express yourself so well and use all the correct words.

I can sympathize with you when you find reading Dickens and Washington Irving difficult and confusing. I do too! These novels were written many years ago. The style of writing in those days was different from today's. We speak and write differently now.

I admire your attempt to read English "classics," but these should not discourage you. I suggest that you improve your English by reading more modern essays, such as those in Great American Short Stories. The articles in English magazines should also help you to understand modern English writing.

With best wishes and warm regards, Bob

▲

Dear Bob,

You cannot imagine how I felt when I found a letter from you in my mailbox. I learned from your words that you are a kind and warm-hearted person. This is not flattery but a genuine belief from the bottom of my heart. I am a student whose hometown is located in a remote area of China.

You gave me a certain kind of praise that has already encouraged me in my English learning process. I have much more confidence now, and I will try my best.

Sincerely, Sema (Beijing)

Unhappiness

Dear Sir,

I read your article by accident. However, it gave me the strength to try to change myself.

I'm an introverted girl. My face will turn red when I speak in front of the class. I am afraid to look people in the eye when I talk with them. I usually don't talk because I cannot choose a suitable topic. I really want to communicate with others and make a lot of friends, but I cannot achieve this goal.

I am accustomed to being a pessimist, and I always lose heart easily. To me, courage and confidence are just distant, abstract words.

I'm very sensitive. I will think about a tiny problem for a long time. The more I think about it, the more terrible I feel. The worst thing is that I usually can't find out a way to overcome the problem.

I'm not pretty. Sometimes I feel like I am sinking in a gray net and can't get out of it. I'm physically healthy, but my heart is bleeding.

So, you see, I could not stay alive if I didn't think I could struggle against the difficulties and have many people help me. I have my parents, my friends, my hobbies, and my goal. I have decided to fight against the difficulties and try to lead a happy life.

Maybe I am in a dark well, and the difficulties and troubles are just the dust. I can shake it off and take a step up.

I know that the key to dealing with my troubles is my character. It's not easy to change one's character. However, give me more encouragement, and I'll try to be more brave and more active to get myself out of the well.

I just want to repeat these words: Shake the dust off and take a step up.

Yours sincerely, Sharon

▲

Dear Sharon,

I am sorry to learn about the unhappiness that you express in your letter. Maybe you are stressing the negatives instead of the positives. There is nothing wrong with being introverted, having difficulty in communicating with others, or feeling a lack of self-confidence. These are often stages of growing up, even though they may make you uncomfortable while you are going through them.

Very often the best way to "find yourself" is to look outward instead of constantly looking inward, by being active and alert and even trying to see the humor of life instead of wasting time beating up on yourself.

You say "it's not easy to change one's character," and you are correct. But maybe you should consider how beautiful your character really is, and what a beautiful person you are. Maybe you should try, several times a day, to repeat to yourself, "I am smart, I am beautiful, I like being who I am." You don't have to change your character. Instead you need to enjoy your character and watch it grow and mature as you develop over the years to come. You have youth, and this is a prize possession. Try to shake off the dust and keep moving forward. I have confidence that you will.

With best wishes, Bob

▲

Dear Bob,

I just wanted to say thank you. When I saw your letter, I really felt excited. When

I read your letter, I burst into tears.

I didn't expect you to send me a letter, because I am used to being a failure. I just wanted to try. However, you sent me a letter. It is the letter itself that is the best encouragement. It tells me that if I try, I may succeed. Thank you for your advice.

I will try to look for the positive things in my life and find delight in myself. The dust, or unhappiness, is a stage of growing up. I'll try to find the advantages of my character, look outward, and see the humor of life. Let's wait and see the result. Thank you again. I really feel happy now because you told me the way to get out of the gray net.

Best wishes, Sharon

The Classroom

Dear Mahya,

I am a faithful reader of *Overseas English*, in which Bob's column is my favorite.

Because I am an English teacher, I have to impart knowledge to students in every class. As you know, today's students do not like it when the teacher repeats the words and sentences from the textbook. This requires me to rack my brain to bring up something new every day. Fortunately, I found Bob's column, which is a rich source for my teaching.

I hope Bob will provide more philosophical stories like the one about a donkey falling into a deserted well. When I shared this story in class, my students liked it very much, and all of us immediately felt encouraged.

I like the contents of the column. Please never let it stop! Thank you very much!

Yours faithfully, Shelley (Shanghai)

▲

Dear Shelley,

It was a joy to know that my column is reaching a classroom in China. I admire your wish to bring new thoughts into your classroom.

I believe that teaching is the most important of all the professions because teachers are preparing for the future and trying to improve it by helping to expand the minds of students. In one sense, we are all teachers, but you have the responsibility of a classroom and the ability to nurture an entire group of young persons. From your letter, I can sense that you take this responsibility seriously, and I admire you for it.

Please never forget the importance of what you are doing. I wish you were my teacher. I am sure that I could learn from you.

With best wishes, Bob

Dear Mahya,

I'm so glad to communicate with you and Bob. I did not respond to Bob when he wrote, "I wish you were my teacher." He is always my teacher. He is so modest.

I've read the introduction to Bob in the August issue, from which I learned that Bob is really somebody, but I think I respect him not for his higher position in society, but for the brilliant mind he shares with us. Please tell Bob I admire him very much!

I have designed a new activity for students in my class. This is based on Bob's column, for we can benefit not only from his beautiful and easily-understood language but also from his intelligent thoughts.

The first story I chose is the one about the donkey, and I also chose some sentences from Bob's column for students to retell. They like this activity very much.

I graduated from Beijing Normal University in 2001 and have been a university teacher in Shanghai since then. With one year's teaching experience, I realize that I have a long way to go to improve my teaching. I hope my students will benefit from my teaching, just like I have benefited from Bob's column.

Best wishes to Bob and you! Shelley (Shanghai)

▲

Dear Mahya,

I like Bob's poem, "Nothings," very much! The last line made me think a lot. What would the world be like if "Me without you" really happened? I will share it with my students.

I don't know how to thank you and Bob. Both of you are so kind to offer me good stories and poems which I can freely use in my class. Maybe trying my best to share Bob's thoughts with my students is the best way to thank both of you!

Thanks again! Shelley (Shanghai)

Dear Shelley,

It was so nice to hear from you again! Thank you for sharing your thoughts with me. Please do not doubt your ability and your passion. I think you have done the very best for yourself. I am looking forward to hearing good news from you.

"My Ideal Universe" can be an interesting topic for your students based on Bob's "The Universe." If your students are willing to try, I would be happy to put their writings in print. The essays do not have to be long. A few sentences with imagination will be good enough. What do you think?

Please take good care of yourself! Mahya

▲

Dear Mahya,

I was really in tears when I read your e-mail. Thank you for your encouragement. I really feel better now. I also tried to seek help from the donkey story. I feel that one "donkey" is not enough to make me feel better; I need more "donkeys." When I think about this, I can't help laughing. "My Ideal Universe" is a good proposal, and I will try it with my students.

Yours faithfully, Shelley (Shanghai)

English Studies

Dear Bob,

When I came across *English Salon*, I wanted to improve my English. When I want to write something in English, I don't know what to say or how to do it well. Every word I write seems so plain. I hope you could give me some advice. I'm looking forward to hearing from you!

Li Shuanghong (Ningxia)

Dear Shuanghong,

Your letter is written in very good English and I understand every word in it.

Please do not worry about writing in plain English. This is the best English. It is when people try to write in fancy English that they make the most mistakes. My only advice to you is to keep trying to write and speak in English. If you do, your language will improve by itself.

Another way of improving is to read as much as possible. English magazines should be helpful. Reading English newspapers and listening to English over the radio or television should also help.

With best wishes, Bob

Professions

Hello Bob,

This time I am writing to you to ask for some information. I know that you are very busy with your work as a scholar. I admire the job that you do. What is your opinion of the jobs that people choose? I think a person should choose the job he wants, but sometimes he may not be choosing the correct job.

Shuanghong (Ningxia)

▲

Dear Shuanghong,

I have been very fortunate in being able to do the kind of "job" I enjoy doing. I wish everyone could enjoy their work. If they did, this world would be a better place to live in.

Some of us are better able to choose what we wish to do with our lives. Generally, it is the more educated persons who have the most choices. My mother once told me (many years ago), "If you enjoy what you are doing, you will never have to work the rest of your life."

It is important to choose work that we enjoy doing. It is also important to understand what our capabilities are. A person with no artistic ability would be making a mistake if he or she chose to make a career of music or painting. Creative persons should be encouraged to do creative work. Persons who like to take responsibility should seek jobs that require high levels of responsibility.

There are also persons who feel more comfortable doing routine tasks. These persons should be encouraged to find jobs that are highly structured and more routinized. There is no "perfect" job which would suit every personality. Just as square pegs should not be pounded into round holes, persons should not be forced to do work that is outside their interests.

Of course, not all of us are in a financial position to choose the job that would fit us perfectly. There are families to be fed, housing and clothing needs, and other financial demands that may force persons to take jobs that may not be perfect for their talents.

I hope that you are searching for the kind of work that will give you a full life.

With best wishes, Bob

Anniversary

Dear Sir,

Today I read your column titled "Love" in *Overseas English*. I like your poem to your wife, Beatrice Herman, very much. In my opinion, only when a man is touched deeply by his marriage can he write such a romantic poem.

You use different comparisons to describe positive relationships between a couple. It is true that relationships change with changing situations. Sometimes the two people help each other and sometimes they protect each other, but basically they should be tolerant, respectful, and trustful of each other. In other words, they should let the other person "be who he or she is." Only in this way can they be the "candle" and the "flame" and live a happy life.

Finally, I have to tell you and your wife that I admire you two for your 60th wedding anniversary, and I believe that my husband and I will celebrate ours in 55 years.

With best wishes, Solely (Chongqing)

▲

Dear Solely,

Beatrice and I were very happy to read your views on marital relationships. We share your views and would look forward to celebrating your 60th wedding anniversary with you. Because of our ages, we probably will not be able to join you, but celebrate anyway.

Marriage is not a simple affair. To be successful, we have found it requires that each person give dignity and respect to the views and the activities of the other. It also requires that, as each person changes, these changes must be understood and appreciated by the other.

We send you and your husband our love and
best wishes, Bob

▲

Dear Mahya,

Thanks for your letter. I forgot to let you know that I enjoyed Bob's letter and yours very much. I even pictured you in my mind: You are a small man with a pair of thick glasses and a warm heart. You needn't tell me if I'm right or not. Let's keep it a secret, ok?

I have to tell you that not only I but also my husband like your name very much, because he has software named Maya. What's your opinion of my English name? It isn't as unique as yours. There's a story behind it.

Have a nice day, Solely (Chongqing)

Dear Solely,

My name, Mahya, sounds like "Maya." I made it up because I like to be unique. Thanks for asking.

I enjoyed receiving your portrait of me. I do have a warm heart but no thick glasses. As for the rest of the portrait, I shall leave it to your vivid imagination.

How did "Solely" originate?

Best regards, Mahya

▲

Dear Mahya,

I'm very glad to know that, in my imagination, you're a warm-hearted man.

When I was a young girl, my father gave me an English name, Solely, and told me, "You have to work hard, and one day you will know the meaning." I found out that solely means lonely after I went to college. I didn't like this name because I wanted to be a happy girl with lots of friends.

As time went by, I realized that my father was right. "Loneliness sometimes makes you blue while making you thoughtful." Do you think so?

My father is very ill. I haven't told him that I like "Solely." I'm far away from him.

I hope my sad story doesn't bother you!

Do you live an American life, sleeping during the day and working at night? Because I noticed that all my e-mails from you were sent in the early morning. Do you know the Chinese saying, "shen ti shi ge ming de ben qian"?

Best wishes, Solely (Chongqing)

▲

Dear Solely,

Thanks for the beautiful story about your name. From each of your letters, I have learned something from you. I like the sentence, "Loneliness sometimes makes you blue while making you thoughtful." Please thank your father for giving you such a meaningful name.

I am sorry to hear that your father is very ill. I hope someone close by is taking good care of him.

I know it's hard for us, as Chinese people, to tell our parents, "I love you," even though we love them deeply. I've always wished that I could say this to my parents before it's too late. In your case, telling your father that you like the name "Solely" can be of great comfort to him. You can't take care of him physically because of the distance between the two of you, but you can share happy thoughts with him and shorten this distance. As a mother of two, I think that an emotional connection means much more than physical presence.

To you, it seems like I am always working at night because of the 13-hour (or more) time difference between the U.S. and China.

Best wishes to you and your father, Mahya

History of Times

Bob,

It has been said that time is the thief of life. It steals our youth, our good days, before we realize it. It is so cruel to see one become old.

Every year, wild geese fly north to spend their summer. Suddenly, they stop when they hear a beautiful song sung by an old man. They ask, "We remember that you were once a young lad. Why are you so old now?" "I really didn't want to become old, but time has made me old."

I understand the old man, and I believe we are insignificant in the long history of time. However, without us, who can make time meaningful?

Sonia (Peijing)

Dear Sonia,

I am pleased to know that you are thinking about some of the most important aspects of life. I share your concern about time and about aging. You and I are thinking along the same lines.

You mention that time "is the thief of life." This is partly true, but it is also true that time is the giver of life. Time gives and time takes away. This is the law of life. Time provides leaves to our trees in the springtime, and then time takes away these same leaves later in the year. Time does steal away our youth, but time also provides us with the years to renew and rejuvenate ourselves after the flush of youth is behind us.

You wrote, "It is so cruel to see one become old." We must remember that old age is a privilege that is denied to many persons. In an important sense, time is life, and years are a gift rather than a burden. Older persons may appear less attractive, but this is only in the eye of the beholder. It is also a result of the youth culture that is being spread throughout the world, especially by active advertising agencies who are promoting products that are supposed to make everyone look younger than he or she is. This is an attempt to deny time, and it always fails in the long run.

I like your story about the wild geese and the old man. I remind you that, in your story, the wild geese heard "a beautiful song sung by an old man." This beautiful song is the song of life. It can be a song filled with memories of the past and hopes for the future.

Best wishes for a long, beautiful, and fruitful life, Bob

Little Woman

Dear Bob,

There are two problems on my mind, and I don't know how to deal with them. I am asking you for advice.

As a child, I liked to play with girls. When I went to middle school, I really did not perceive that I had become effeminate, which followed me into high school. Now, a lot of boys in my class laugh at me and call me "Little Woman." I don't know how to deal with it.

I am very nervous about speaking in public, even answering questions in the classroom. I often tell myself, "It's nothing! Cool it! I'll be the best!" Could you tell me how I can be calm on these occasions?

Yours sincerely, Steven (Shangrao, Jiangxi)

▲

Dear Steven,

From the way you describe your problems, I feel that you will outgrow them as you grow and mature. Children find it fun to tease others who are a bit different from them. Very often children can be sadistic, and they like to show their superiority in antagonistic ways.

Each of us is an individual. No two persons are exactly alike. It requires some maturity to understand and accept this. If you can keep your cool, believe in yourself, and avoid confrontations, I believe that your life will be easier and filled with new friends.

With warm regards and best wishes, Bob

Another Proverb

Dear Bob,

After reading your column, "Proverbs," I am very puzzled by the sentence, "You can't saw sawdust." What does this mean?

Yours respectfully, Tian (Xiamen)

▲

Dear Tian,

It is always a pleasure to share thoughts with our Chinese readers. You ask me about the meaning of one of my favorite proverbs: "You can't saw sawdust." This says that after a log (or piece of wood) is turned into sawdust, it can never be turned back into a log.

The deeper meaning tells us that after an event happens, we cannot go back and change it. It tells us that, instead of looking back, we must try to look ahead. I have found this very useful in my life. Instead of looking back to what I might have done, it is better to look ahead to what I can do next.

I hope this explains my proverb. Thank you for your inquiry. This is how we learn from each other.

With warm regards and best wishes, Bob

▲

Dear Ms. Zhang,

I am very grateful to have received the e-mails from you and Bob. I did not think that I would receive them in such a short time. Thank you very much.

I want to say thanks to Bob. After reading his e-mail, I was very moved. What he said to me is what I have been thinking about. Time is passing so quickly, and I will be 28. I feel very terrified. I look at my face very carefully in the mirror. And ask myself what I have done during these years. Then, I tell myself that we can't stop the movement of time, and we needn't regret anything. What we can do is to grasp the present time. I thank Bob for his poem, "Elegy to Time." It really enlightened me and will always do so. Also, I thank him for explaining the proverb, "We can't saw sawdust." I know we can't, and I will never try to saw sawdust. Please send my best regards to Bob.

Yours respectfully, Tian (Xiamen)

▲

Hello, Dr. Robert Herman,

You are right that humor is the shortest bridge between people. I have a funny story for you.

There were two birds. One had a green face, and the other had a red face. You would need one bullet to shoot the green-faced one and two bullets to shoot the red-faced one. One day, a man killed both of them but used only two bullets. Do you know why?

The clever man shot the green-faced bird first. When the red-faced one saw the dead green-faced bird, its face turned green from fear. Then the man shot the bird with one bullet. Please tell me what you think about this story.

Your friend, Vivien (Xian, Shanxi)

Dear Vivien,

I enjoyed reading your letter, and I especially enjoyed getting a new joke—all the way from China! Your story about the green-faced bird is very funny in America, and I will share it among my friends. Of course, I shall tell them it came from you.

Thank you for writing to me. We are far apart in distance, but we seem to be close in humor. Keep laughing, and please keep telling funny stories.

Respectfully yours, Bob

Dear Mahya,

I am happy to hear from you. I want to know if it is very hard for a Chinese to survive in a foreign country. My brother is going to study in the U.S. I am worried about him. He is very smart, but he has a bad temper. He seems abnormal.

Where are you from? Hope your family has a happy life.

Yours, Vivien (Xian, Shanxi)

Dear Vivien,

Thanks for writing to me. My hometown is Hefei, Anhui. My parents, my two brothers, and their families live there.

Living in the U.S. is, of course, different from living in China, since the two countries have their own traditions, cultures, laws, beliefs, and even food. But as a human being, especially a smart one like your brother, one can adjust one's life accordingly wherever one goes.

From your letter, I could tell that you are very loving towards your Dear brother. Please do not worry. Instead of being troubled by his departure and future, you should put more trust in him and remember not to label him as having personality problems or being "abnormal." You can spend time with him by talking to him before and after he leaves. Help him to believe in himself, and let him know that he is loved. Once a person knows that others care about him, he will be more aware of his behavior and actions. More importantly, he will be more confident when dealing with obstacles. And please remember that love is contagious!

So, Vivien, try to think about all the nice times that you and your brother have spent together. Tell him that you are proud of him, and wish him the best on his new adventure. Also, if possible, you should share Bob's column with him, since Bob's thoughts are very meaningful. I think that's all he needs from you.

It is nice to share my point of view with you.

Best wishes, Mahya

▲

Dear Mahya,

Your advice is really good! I will follow your advice and believe in him. I am guessing that you are Chinese and Bob's secretary.

It is hard to make foreign friends. I like to chat online, but I cannot understand Americans. I do not know how to deal with Westerners. I think they are queer. I am embarrassed when I talk to them. I do not know why.

Can you help me or pass my letter to Dr. Herman?

Yours, Vivien (Xian, Shanxi)

▲

Dear Vivien,

I read Mahya's thoughtful response to you. I hope you will take her advice. Mahya is a warm, sensitive person who has had experience in both the Chinese and the American cultures.

In your letter, you mention that you do not know how to deal with Westerners and that you think they are sometimes "queer." Because Westerners come from a different culture and may look or dress or act a bit differently, I can understand your confusion. Please keep in mind that all of us, whether we are Chinese or Americans or Europeans, are very similar and share the most basic aspects of life.

We all desire food, shelter, good health, education, employment, personal safety, and the dignity of being human. We are all thinking persons. We are all born, we all live, and we all die on the same Earth. We all want to achieve our goals. We are also subject to the same advantages and disadvantages of the galloping technology which threatens to change our lives forever. We share so much regardless of our color, our language, or the country we live in.

When you are with Westerners, please try to keep in mind all these, and many more, similarities instead of looking at our differences. In playing the piano, for example, there are white keys and black keys, and it is by using all the keys that we are able to achieve a harmony. I believe the same is true for Asians, Americans, Africans, and everyone else. By celebrating our shared goals and by understanding and enjoying our differences, we should make this a better planet to live and work on.

Instead of viewing others as "queer," maybe it would be better to consider what can be learned from them in terms of both similarities and differences.

With warm regards, Bob

The Heart

Dear Bob,

I was happy when I read your article, "The Universe," in *Overseas English*. It would be amazing if I could recreate the world.

If I could recreate the world, I would let children be born and grow like plants. If adults want a child, they would have to buy some kind of seeds and plant them in a garden. In this case, the father and the mother would make the same amount of effort, instead of having the mother suffer the great pain. Maybe sexual discrimination would decrease.

After the child grows up, it have the right to choose whatever it wanted to be. It could be a rabbit, a rat, a sheep, a dog, a lily flower, or heather. Appearance, sex, and all other things that seem so important today would make no sense. The only thing that matters would be the heart, the pure love between people (or creatures). It would be so beautiful that a flying sparrow could fall in love with a swimming goldfish, and a red rose with a jellyfish. There would be no barrier to love. Wouldn't that be beautiful?

That is the feeling that I want to share with you. I hope you write back.

Yours, Vivian (Xian, Shanxi)

▲

Dear Vivian,

I admire your imagination and for joining me in trying to think about our Universe. It is fun to speculate on how we could improve it if we had all the tools.

I adore your idea of buying seeds and letting them grow into children. How wonderful to think of sparrows falling in love with goldfish, and roses with jellyfish. This would be natural love and no sexual preferences.

Your thoughts reach deep into my soul. You are right in saying that sex is less important than pure love between people. I don't know your profession, but I urge you to try writing more of your ideas for publication so they can be shared with others in China.

With warm regards and best wishes, Bob

▲

Dear Bob,

Thanks for your letter. Your letters always make me happy.

English is my major. I really love writing, but I am not skilled at it. I think having a pure heart and a good sense of observation are the most important elements in writing.

Yours, Vivian (Xian, Shanxi)

Shattered Dreams

Bob,

I have a serious problem in my life and eagerly need your advice and help.

I will graduate this year. All of my classmates have already found jobs, but I haven't. I feel terrible. Why am I so unlucky? I just can't believe it. I feel like all I learned has amounted to nothing. I have a good command of spoken English, but it has not helped in my job hunt. I feel terrible. Half a year has passed.

These days, I wonder about the causes of my failure. I consult my teachers, my classmates, and my family members. I have changed much. All my dreams were shattered by the serious reality. I found out that success depends upon many factors! I should change my outlook and try my best to pursue my ideal life.

Yours, Vincent (Wuhan, Hubei)

Bob,

I hope you read my first letter. Now I am sorry to tell you that another terrible thing has happened in my life. I lost my best friend! He lied to me, and the whole thing has caused me deep sorrow.

You don't know how hard it is for me to get through this period of time. I try my best to forget about him. I don't know whether I can forget him or not. I feel too tired.

I hope you can give me some advice on life!

Yours, Vincent (Wuhan, Hubei)

▲

Bob,

Why does the spring come so late? I have waited for too long. While hunting for a job, I learned to think deeply about life. Now I have a fresh new outlook on the outside world.

The first step is for me to enter society. I encountered a big setback. I need to learn a lot! I need your encouragement and I need your advice, my friend!

Whatever I do now, I should not regret it years later.

Yours sincerely, Vincent (Wuhan, Hubei)

▲

Dear Vincent,

Thank you for all of your letters. They touch me deeply. You seem to be such a thoughtful person with a broad outlook on life and its problems. I am glad that you are sharing your problems and your feelings with me. You write with much passion.

It is easy for me to understand your frustrations about finding a good job that matches your talents. I hope you will not give up too soon or get discouraged. A person who is discouraged is often not as attractive as a person who looks at life happily. You are correct when you tell me that success depends upon a lot of factors. It certainly does. It depends upon a person's personality, temperament, and abilities. It also depends upon the job market. Even the most brilliant person cannot find a job if there are no jobs available.

Then there is always the **chance** factor. Life is often governed by chains of chances, the luck of being at a certain time or a certain place or meeting certain persons. These chance factors cannot be planned. I hope that they favor you in your search. From your letter I can tell that you have an excellent command of English and that you will graduate from university. These are two impressive accomplishments and should help you toward a successful future.

I am sorry to read about you losing your best friend. This can be sad, but it might also give you good experience in understanding other persons. Life consists mostly of relationships. How we experience these relationships and what we learn from them will be major parts of our lives. Of course, time is an important element to consider, and very often the passage of time will soften our feelings after we suffer from a detached relationship. I hope this is true for you.

Your last letter is very heartening for me. I am proud of you for finding a "fresh new outlook on the outside world". These are your words, and they express such wisdom. You seem to have made the most of your experiences. I applaud you and I wish more of our readers would be able to share your attitude. To be able to see life from a distance is a gift that you are developing. This is so important for your social and for your mental being. Life is a blessing that we all share. What we do with this blessing will determine how successful our lives are.

With best wishes for a successful career and a happy life, Bob

▲

Bob,

Thank you very much! I know I should face difficulties bravely.

I have good news and bad news to tell you. The good news is that a foreign trade company in Beijing finally promised to hire me. The bad news is that the manager keeps delaying the date of my enrollment, and I am afraid she doesn't want to recruit me.

The problem is that if I wait, I will lose many other opportunities. I feel terrible again. Would you please give some advice?

Yours, Vincent (ZengJia)

▲

Dear Vincent,

Thank you for asking my advice about your job situation. Sorry, but I am unable to help you because I am not familiar with the business situation. I guess you need a balance between being patient and being impatient.

Best wishes, Bob

Friendship

Dear Bob,

Hey, I am a girl from China. I am writing to you because I have a problem with one of my friends, Yan Meng. I know she wrote to you and got your reply. We were good friends for a long time, and she was my best friend.

One evening, we began to quarrel while we were chatting online. I was devastated. After that, I was crying all the time. The next day, I called her and tried to explain.

Now we are still friends, but not as good as before. I cannot understand why. I think that our friendship is almost gone.

March 9th is her birthday. I want to surprise her. I hope that we can be best friends again! So Bob, tell me what to do! Help me, please?! Please reply!

Weiqing (Luoyang, Henan)

Dear Weiqing,

I am sorry that you have a problem with your friendship, but this might be a good experience for you. It is not easy to make new friends. We treasure the friends we have and hate to lose them.

If I were you, I would speak with Yan Meng and tell her how sorry you are about the misunderstanding. Tell her how important her friendship is to you. I feel sure she will understand. And please give her my congratulations for her birthday on March 9. Maybe the best "surprise" you can give her is a big **hug**. And while you doing this, please give her a hug from me.

With warm regards and best wishes, Bob

⚊⚊⚊⚊⚊ ▲ ⚊⚊⚊⚊⚊

Bob,

Thank you for the reply! You are really a kind man. Best wishes to you. Today is Yan Meng's birthday, and I will give her a hug! I hope we can still be best friends.

Please keep in touch.

God bless you, Weiqing (Luoyang, Henan)

⚊⚊⚊⚊⚊ ▲ ⚊⚊⚊⚊⚊

Dear Mahya and Bob,

Thanks for the surprise!

Weiqing already told you about what happened between us. It was really a misunderstanding. I was also very sorry for that. Everything is ok now.

On my 14th birthday, she explained her feelings to me and gave me a very big hug. Wow, that was wonderful. Then she showed me the e-mails. This was the **best** and the most unforgettable birthday present I ever got.

And next day, we shared a meal at McDonald's and had a long chat. We decided to work on websites together. This will be a good chance to improve our friendship.

We have always been best friends, and we will always be! Thanks a lot!

Yours, Yan Meng (Luoyang, Henan)

▲

Dear Meng,

Your beautiful letter just arrived. Thank you for writing. I feel the hug over here. You see that even a big ocean like the Pacific isn't big enough to stop a hug.

I hope you will keep the hugs going and that they will be accompanied by lots of conversation and understanding.

With best wishes, Bob

Grammar

Dear Bob,

I am a university student in Wuhan. I like learning English, but I have some trouble with the language. I forgot most of the grammar that I have learned. I was told that grammar is not important.

Please tell me how to learn English well and how important grammar is. This is a big problem for all English learners in China.

Yours, Liu Wangxi (Wuhan, Hubei)

▲

Dear Wangxi,

Learning English is not easy. Learning English grammar is even harder. There is no easy way to do it. The best advice is to study, imitate, and practice. Knowing the rules is important if you want a full command of the language.

Whether grammar is important depends on how you wish to use your English. For conversation, grammar may not be as important as it would be if you are attempting to write in English. I believe there are millions of Americans who converse in English every day yet are ignorant of the grammar rules.

I admire every Chinese student who is trying to learn English. It is not a "rational" language. It is changing constantly, and the spoken language is a bit different from the written language. My best wishes to you. From your letter, I think you have a good beginning.

Best wishes, Bob

▲

Dear Ms. Zhang,

I am majoring in several subjects. As a college student, I would like to work in Nanjing someday,

In reality, my family is not rich. I have three or more years of study, because I want to be a postgraduate. There is a long way for me to go. Would you mind giving me some advice?

Respectfully, Chang Wei (Hefei, Anhui)

▲

Dear Wei,

Mahya has asked me to respond to your letter to her.

I admire your ambition to become a postgraduate. Coming from a family without a lot of financial resources may be a handicap, but it can also be a blessing. In your case, I believe that it has given you even more incentive to succeed. From your letter, I can tell that you write well, that you are a serious student, that you want to succeed, and that you do not hesitate to ask for advice. All of these characteristics are going to blend into a very fine future for you. A few years from now, I expect to hear about how good a career you have achieved.

With warm regards and best wishes, Bob

Knowledge

Dear Mr. Herman,

After reading your article and the introduction by Mahya, I learned a lot from your work, your profound knowledge, logical thinking, and high energy for life.

After graduating from a nursing school in 1989, I have never been able to find satisfying work or earn enough money. I worked in a hospital temporarily and got little pay and no benefits. Facing the unfair fate, I attempted to show my abilities, but I failed and failed. I left my job last year and began to concentrate on English studies with the hope of going abroad. It will not be easy for me to go abroad, because I need more than 80,000 RMB to support myself.

Why is it so difficult for me? Could you please tell me what I should do? I would appreciate any reply that you could give me at your convenience.

Yours faithfully, Wendy (Jinan, Shandong)

▲

Dear Wendy,

Your letter shows that you are a very thoughtful person. It is not easy to give vocational advice from such a distance, especially because I am not familiar with the profession of nursing in China.

I believe that nursing and teaching are the most honorable professions. They are of the greatest benefit to all our fellow citizens. The influence of a nurse, like that of a teacher, can last for many years. In America, we have a shortage of skilled nurses. This is unfortunate because we have so many persons who are in need of nursing care. The nurses that I have met during my various illnesses have been the most caring and nurturing women. They contributed much joy to my life and survival.

Have you tried to find places in China where nursing care is needed? With a population that is growing and aging, it seems that the demand for nurses should be increasing. Older persons especially need help from skilled nurses. Is it possible that you can find places to get training in treatment of older patients?

The need for home health care in America is also increasing rapidly. Have you tried to explore this possibility in China? Are there government agencies that could help you to find work in nursing care? Your English might be a help.

With best wishes, Bob

▲

Dear Bob,

I was very glad to read your letter today. I do not know how to express my feeling. Thank you for your reply and help.

I have found an agency that can help me go to Glasgow as a nurse, but I am not sure if I can believe the agency. I do not know if everything in the UK is as perfect as they say. Have you heard anything about nursing in the UK? Could you please tell me what specific work they do? May I know your opinion of my English? Thanks again.

Your faithful, Wendy (Jinan, Shandong)

▲

Dear Wendy,

Here are my quick thoughts. If I were you, I would ask myself what my passion is. If you love being a nurse, you can stay in your field and try working at a big hospital with better benefits. In some big cities, there are Friendship Hospitals, where bilingual nurses are needed. I think you are a very smart person, and you have much potential.

China is such a huge country with endless opportunities. After China joined the WTO, many foreigners have started their businesses in China. If you feel that you can't find a satisfying job in China, there is a slim chance of finding a better job somewhere else. In addition, to avoid financial problems, staying in your own country **may** be the smartest choice. Almost every other country is experiencing severe unemployment problems.

Best wishes, Mahya

▲

Dear Mahya,

Bob's letter has given me some useful information indeed, but your advice makes me a little bit confused. It is true that China is such a huge country with endless opportunities because many foreigners have started their businesses there, but do you know what nurses do? Do you know how much money an industrious nurse can get? It is very unfair.

I like my work very much, although sometimes I cannot enjoy it because of the unfair salary.

Yours honestly, Wendy (Jinan, Shandong)

▲

Dear Wendy,

I appreciate the time you took to write to Mahya and me. Unfortunately, I am not familiar with the nursing situation in Glasgow or anywhere else in the UK. Whether to move from China to UK is a big decision and must be a very personal one for you. It must involve many considerations in addition to the nursing possibilities. When we move over such a long distance, we must consider separation from family and friends, different climate and language, as well as a new culture and tradition. These, and other considerations, may be handicaps to moving, or they may be incentives. In either case, they should be considerations when one is thinking of such a large change.

As you know, I believe that nursing is one of the most important professions that anyone could have. It is sad that the financial rewards for being a nurse are not sufficient when compared with other occupations. This is true in almost every country. It does seem unfair. Perhaps in the future, with growing demands for nursing care, this can be changed.

In the meantime, please continue to use your best judgment and consider all factors when contemplating a move to a new environment. Your English is excellent. Try to keep using it.

Respectfully yours, Bob

▲

Dear Bob,

First, I want to say Merry Christmas and Happy New Year! I hope you stay happy and healthy forever.

Please give my greetings to Mahya. I couldn't have contacted you without her warmhearted and generous help. 祝愿她：好人一生平安. If she is Chinese, she will understand. If she isn't, just send it back to me.

Yours honestly, Wendy (Jiana, Shandong)

▲

Dear Wendy,

Thank you for your greetings. On a personal level, this is a happy holiday time. On a global level, it is filled with unhappiness when I think of all the misery on this planet. We have the resources to eliminate much of this misery, but we do not use them for this purpose.

My colleague, Mahya, is a Chinese woman who is kind and generous and extremely bright. Without her, I could not write these columns in *Overseas English* and *English Salon*. I know that she treasures all of the letters that are sent to her.

Our best wishes to you for 2003 and for many happy years ahead. We hope that we have a better world to look forward to.

Respectfully yours, Bob

Affirmations

Dear Bob,

I was so glad to see your letter today. I read your column, "Proverbs." I like it, but I cannot understand two of them:

1. Some people feel the rain; other people just get wet.
2. Even a blind hog can find an acorn once in while.

I am already 32 years old, but I want to change my life. There are only a few chances for me. I have confidence to face reality. What would you do if your friends always warn you about your choices?

Thanks for Mahya's kindness and her introduction to you in *Overseas English*. May I have some information about her? I am just curious.

Yours honestly, Wendy (Jinan, Shandong)

▲

Dear Wendy,

Regarding the two proverbs, sometimes they are not easy to explain. Proverbs are bits of wisdom which often have different meanings for different persons.

When it is raining, some people feel the rain and other people only get wet. To me, this means that if rain is only getting wet to one person, then that person is thinking in narrow terms, of himself and perhaps his clothes. If another person feels the rain, the meaning is a bit different. To this person, the rain may have many effects – it may feel cleansing, or invigorating, or even nostalgic. This interpretation shows a broader perspective toward rain. To this person, rain is more than merely getting wet.

Blind hogs do find acorns once in a while. I interpret this to mean that luck may be an element in some achievements. We often stumble on some chance occurrence which can produce benefits for us such as meeting a particular person or being at a certain spot at a certain time.

You ask about the wisdom of changing your life. Of course, life is in constant change whether we encourage it or not. How much to change our personal life is a hard choice for each of us. Sometimes we become comfortable in our present environment with our friends and family and do not like the prospect of changing. Other times, we wish for more excitement, more mobility, more challenge in our lives. In either case, one's personality, temperament, and experience will decide whether it is better to change one's lifestyle or to keep the present one.

Change can be threatening or exhilarating, depending on the person and the situation. Changing one's life presents both opportunities and risks. My only advice is to think about the person you are. What are your values, your ambitions, your tolerances (for change), your hopes, and your fears? Then bring these together and consider all the possible changes that might be available to you. The next step is to weigh the rewards and the risks of making each of the possible changes.

I am glad that you asked about Mahya. She is not only my brilliant editor; she is also my colleague and closest friend. She is also my mentor. It was Mahya who asked me to become a writer for *Overseas English* and for *English Salon*, and I have enjoyed this role very much. Mahya and her husband, Trent, are now living in California and have two beautiful daughters, Jenny and Anne. They lead active lives and return to China frequently to visit with their families. Mahya is a warm, kind, and generous woman. My personal comment about her is that if there were more Mahyas in this world it would be a much better place for all of us to live in.

Best wishes and warm regards, Bob

Dear Wendy,

Since writing to you, I have given more thought to the proverb about blind hogs finding acorns, and I think it has a deeper meaning than only luck. It means that with enough persistence, we may succeed. Even a hog that is blind can find acorns if it persists long enough. Thank you for making me think more about this.

With warm regards, Bob

Translations

Dear Bob and Mahya,

Please help me to analyze and translate the following sentences. Thank you very much!

Someone once said, "What goes around comes around. Work like you don't need the money. Love like you have never been hurt. Dance like nobody is watching."

Yan Wf

▲

Dear Wf,

Mahya sent me your letter asking for a translation and analysis of some "American" phrases. Unfortunately, I am not capable of translating. Sorry. But here is how I interpret the phrase that you sent:

"What goes around comes around" means that life consists of many repetitions. To me, it also means that if we give to others, others will give to us.

"Work like you don't need the money" means that we should enjoy what we are doing and not work at something unpleasant just because we are paid to do it. Of course, this is a privilege which many persons are not in a position to enjoy. The need to earn money to feed ourselves and our families often requires us to work at tasks that might not be our first choice. This also means that we should work hard at what we are doing, and that the financial reward should not be the only incentive.

"Love like you've never been hurt" means that we should still retain our ability to love, even though we may have had hurtful experiences in loving in the past. We must be careful not to let the past harm the present in our relationships with other persons.

"Dance like nobody's watching" means that we should be ourselves and not behave only because somebody is watching us. Our lives should not be inhibited by being afraid of what others may think. The common advice might be to "follow your bliss" and to follow your own instincts.

Thank you for your inquiry. Others may have different interpretations, but these are the best I can provide. Please keep on thinking and questioning.

With warm regards, Bob

Tutoring

Dear Robert,

I am a sophomore at an unknown university. I like English very much. I passed the CET-4 with a score of 88.

I want to be a tutor and to teach children English. To my disappointment, the parents who called me did not want to hire me because I am not from a normal college. My room-mates told me to cheat and to say that I am from a normal university. I am confused. I love children, and I am also will-ing to help them. If the parents don't give me a chance, there is no way that I can be a tutor.

Why do people merely judge my ability and knowledge from the name of my college? What should I do?

Now I am tiptoeing with expectations of hearing from you.

Best wishes to you, Xiazi (Naijing, Jiangsu)

Dear Xiazi,

I think that it is wonderful that you wish to share your learning of English with children. As a tutor, you are in a position to help children, and there is no greater occupation than helping children to learn.

I admit being puzzled over the reaction of parents to your university credentials. Unfortunately, I am not familiar with the university structure in China. I believe that you must continue to be honest and not lie about which university you belong to. This is important for your own integrity, and it would be unfair to mislead anyone.

The name of a university should mean much less than the quality of its students. It is sad that we classify universities and then judge their students on the basis of this classification. To a lesser extent, this also happens here in America. It is assumed that students at Harvard or MIT are superior to students at other American universities. This is not a true assumption.

My only suggestion is that you continue to try to reason with parents. Try to convince them that the quality of the person is more important than the quality of a university. The motivation you have in wanting to work with children is of greatest importance.

Mahya is more familiar with the Chinese university system than I am. She may have some further advice for you.

With best wishes and warm regards, Bob

▲

Dear Xiazi,

Bob asked me to add my comments. I always get meaningful messages from Bob's letters. I liked Bob's wise suggestion "to be honest . . . This is important for your own integrity."

I understand your situation: If you do not lie, you may never have a chance to meet any of your potential students.

If I were you, I would answer calls from parents with confidence. "My CET-4 is almost 90. English is my favorite subject, and teaching kids English is my dream job because I love English, and, more importantly, I love children. I would like to meet your child and give him (or her) the first two lessons for free . . ." Please remember, before answering any phone calls, to let the phone ring two times and to practice your smile.

Let me know if you become a tutor.

Best wishes, Mahya

▲

Dear Editor,

I was overjoyed to hear from both Bob and you. Thank you very much for your sincere and advisable suggestions.

I have been fully occupied with preparing for upcoming tests, so you might not hear if I become a tutor this semester. There is no doubt that I will be more confident in the future. Whenever I am confronted with difficulties, I will remember what you and Bob told me, and I am sure I will do well in everything.

Please convey my gratitude to Bob.

Yours sincerely, Xiazi

Life is Complicated

Dear Bob,

I am a sophomore in college. I am so eager to write to you after reading your article about life.

I had a happy childhood under my parents' safeguard. I thought everyone was a kind individual. However, my college life makes me puzzled.

Some of our grades depend on a professor. If you have good relationship with the professor, you will get a high grade. It is unfair.

Why do beautiful girls and handsome boys become class leaders? College is as complex as society. What is the difference between college students and other members of society?

Perhaps my opinions are so puerile.

Yours, Xuefen (Fujian)

▲

Dear Xuefen,

Life is a complicated matter, and your letter shows that you are learning much about it. As you point out, life consists of relationships, and our relationships with each other can be confusing and many times irrational.

How we view each other depends on many factors. Physical appearance is only one, but it is this one that seems to be on your mind. Your experience in college may or may not be universal. I do understand it. In an age of television and movies, physical appearance seems to dominate our thinking. Advertising makes us wish that we looked better or that we looked younger. It makes us believe that our lives depend on how we appear physically. This is sad. It is done to sell products. We are not "products." We are persons.

It is good that we take some pride in our appearance, but it is not good if we allow this to dominate our lives. If your college gives advantages to the better looking students, this is unfortunate. Please don't worry too much about it. I have found that, later in life, the students who study hard are the ones who hire the students who are the best looking.

It is also true that relationships with faculty can determine some success in college. Professors are generally impressed by students who are warm and friendly toward them. In this way, colleges are mirrors of the wider society. We tend to favor persons who favor us.

You are obviously a sensitive young person who wishes to succeed by studying hard. Please don't change. What you learn will become more important than how you look.

Best wishes for a successful future, Bob

Stagnation

Hi, Bob!

I want to be your friend. I like English, and I even talk with foreigners in my dreams.

I am an unmarried Chinese girl. I have a job, but I often feel dull and have no enthusiasm for life. I don't know how to love or how to find beauty in life. I am always afraid of losing my job.

Yaping (Huaian)

▲

Dear Yaping,

I am sorry to hear that you have lost your "enthusiasm for life." This should be impossible. Of course, life can be hard, and it can be unjust and even irrational. It is often unfair and unreasonable. However, it is also brief and the only life we have on this earth.

Our lives are usually full of obstacles. Sometimes, it is our job that is unpleasant or a love that was not returned, or the death of someone close to us. When we face an obstacle, the best course is to decide how to overcome it. Some obstacles are harder to deal with than others. Some take much longer to cope with. From your letter, I assume that your major problem concerns your job.

I believe that the best way to find a job or to keep a job is to be enthusiastic, not to lose your enthusiasm. There is much beauty in life just as there is much sorrow, and each of us has a responsibility to find his or her own beauty. Please look for yours. Being positive and being as cheerful as you can should make it easier to find and keep a job. Remember that a smile is the easiest way to improve your appearance.

Yaping, my friend, you are more important than your problem. Please keep this in mind and deal with your obstacle in the best and most positive way you can.

With best wishes, Bob

Dear Bob,

Thank you very much. I appreciate your concern for me. In fact, things are not as serious as you imagine.

This time I want to ask you another question. Should an older girl who has not found her ideal lover continue to wait or get married?

Yaping (Huaian)

▲

Dear Yaping,

The response to your recent letter is very easy for me. I believe that we are born to love, and this desire never leaves us. Some people find it hard to show their love. Other people hide their love behind a drive to achieve power or money. But the love must still be there. Everyone has it.

An older girl, as you mention, should never give up her feelings of love, and she should never give up trying to find someone to share these feelings with her. Whether she should wait for a "perfect" love or marry in the hope that this love will turn out to be "perfect" is a very personal decision. It is not an unusual decision. There are often social or financial pressures to marry. These must be considered along with family concerns. I believe that millions of women, both young and old, are facing this decision. I hope that all of them make the right choice.

With warm regards, Bob

Advice

Dear Bob,

Thank you very much. Your article about time woke me up. You wrote, "Time is the essence of life. How we spend our time tells other people who we are. We define ourselves by our use of time." Your comments are to the point. Time is so important to each one of us. We should cherish it and use it wisely and efficiently.

Zhang Yong (Hubei)

▲

Dear Yong,

I am pleased that you value time as much as I do. Time is a treasure granted to each of us, and I feel sorry that so much of it is wasted by so many of our fellow human beings.

With warm regards and best wishes, Bob

▲

Hello, Sir,

This is the first time I have written to you. I wonder if you would give me some advice on how to get an ideal job. Should I stay on campus to get a better academic diploma in order to find a better job in the future, or should I hunt for a job now? Should I go far away from my university and my hometown to find a job?

Zengjia (Wuhan, Hubei)

Choices

Dear Zengjia,

You raise a question that is in the minds of millions of students throughout the world. It is the question of whether it is better to stay on campus and get more education or to get a job.

The answer to this question is like the answer to most other questions and can be stated in three simple words: It all depends.

There is no universal answer which suits all persons in all situations. There are obvious advantages to staying in school and obvious advantages to going out into the work world.

The argument for staying on campus is that more education should help to broaden one's perspective on life and eventually lead to a higher position and a larger income. This, of course, depends on the quality of the education and the path it is leading to. Sometimes staying in school can be an excuse for not going out into the world of work. The value of school education should be weighed against the value of the education that is available outside the schoolroom. Sometimes we can learn more away from the campus by meeting other persons and learning from them. We can also learn from our work and become more skilled. This can lead to promotions and higher incomes and more responsibility.

So, Zengjia, it is a matter of choosing between two alternatives, and much depends upon your own personality and interests. Some persons find the campus life stimulating and nurturing. Others find it dull and irrelevant. Some find the work world exciting and invigorating. Others find it too competitive.

My best wishes are with you. I can appreciate how hard this choice can be, but years from now, I anticipate that you will feel that you have made the best choice.

With warm regards, Bob

▲

Dear Bob,

Thanks for your reply. I appreciate your advice and blessings. You gave me a wise answer. I not only learned the right attitude but also confirmed that I should use my own mind to decide my own future!

Thank you very much! It's really a pleasure to write to you. I hope we can communicate in the future.

Zengjia (Wuhan, Hubei)

English Lessons

Dear Bob,

I am a reader of *Overseas English* and *English Salon*. I love your columns very much. From your writing, I can tell that you are a perfect person.

I am a senior in high school. I love English best. May I ask you a question? Which is better to say, "hotel California" or "California hotel"? Thank you!

Best wishes! Zhao (Longshang, Sichuan)

▲

Dear Zhao,

Language is such an important feature of life, and I admire your ability to use both Chinese and English. I imagine that English is a very difficult language to learn. It changes rapidly with new words added and other words becoming obsolete. Our idioms are confusing, and I am always interested in reading about them in publications.

In response to your question, we refer to "the California hotel," or "the hotel in California." We would say "Hotel California" only if we were referring to a specific hotel with that name.

I hope you will continue with your English studies. You have such a fine beginning.

With warm regards, Bob

▲

Dear Mahya and Bob,

I was surprised to receive your letter! I thought you were too busy to write to me. Thanks.

I introduced your columns to several friends. They said they also love you and your columns. They said you have provided them with the best way to learn English, along with some beautiful poems to enjoy.

As an American citizen, what do you think of the war in Iraq? What effect will it have on the financial markets after the war? Do you think the U.S. will win the war against Iraq?

I want to study abroad in the fall in 2004. Can you give me some advice on how to apply to universities?

Best wishes! Zhao (Longshang, Sichuan)

▲

Dear Zhao,

You can find information about U.S. colleges on the Internet, in bookstores, or at libraries (at your local colleges). I also find that English Corner, an English conversation place every Sunday morning in every big city in China, is the best place to get up-to-date information on studying abroad.

It is very easy to find the websites of almost all of the U.S. colleges online. You can write to them, just like you wrote to me, and ask them to mail you application forms. You might even be able to apply online, if you are lucky. Please be aware that you have to take a few exams (such as the TOEFL and GRE) before you send your application to any college. It can be time-consuming to figure out which college suits you the best, but it is worth the time and energy. Knowing what you want and also knowing what a college can offer you are the keys to success. To improve the chance of acceptance, most students apply to three or more colleges at the same time.

Do you have any friends who know others at American colleges? If you do, ask your friend. Your friend will probably be able to help you than I can. Good luck.

Best wishes, Mahya

▲

Dear Zhao,

I am always pleased when our Chinese friends read my columns.

I appreciate your questions concerning the present war with Iraq, but I prefer not to comment on this sensitive subject. I urge everyone in every country to try to find ways to bring peace to this troubled world. There are many paths to peace. Let us hope that the best one will be found.

With warm regards and best wishes for a
peaceful future, Bob

Pessimism

Dear Bob,

I was very upset during the National Day. As a freshman, my vacation never touched a slight happiness.

I was spending the tasteless holidays with my grandpa in a wonderful city Nanjing. But turn out, it's such kind of lousy days that drives me nuts. My grandpa, a retired professor, teased me with no reason. . . . He made me feel as if I were a real bastard. He claimed that it makes no sense that a freshman learns computer lessons and foreign languages. . . . All these damn words struck me deeply like a heavy axe. He even criticized the whole society with cynical words and nothing in his eyes really rocks except himself. I guess he's so weird until I heard something from my mama, an "appalling" fact: it's 'cause my grandpa had no chance to get further promotion in his university that he felt unfair and conveyed these feelings to me.

Well, from my point of view, I'm not the babe in the woods certainly. It's no use criticizing the world, I guess, that everything is the hell, anymore than everything is not perfect as we hope.

I'm really devastated when I heard such words from my grandpa, which totally damage his respectable figure in my mind. The vocation is on, while I never give a damn about it! Dear Bob, could you tell me how to handle this? I'm waiting for your reply anxiously.

Yours respectfully, Nicole Shuhong

Dear Nicole,

Thank you for writing to me. You certainly do have problems, and one of them seems to be you! Your letter shows me that you seem to be majoring in discontent. Nothing seems to appeal to you. You tell me that you are dissatisfied with the University, and with your grandpa. Wow! That is a lot of discontent to spread around. I hope things are not as bad as you say they are. And I hope you grow up with the understanding that perhaps the fault is with you and not with everyone else.

I am fascinated by your description of your grandpa Grandpas can be annoying or they can be fun. I am a grandpa, and I am both. Maybe your grandpa enjoys teasing you. He has earned the right. Maybe he was treated unfairly at a University. So what! This is his problem. Maybe he likes to shift some of his anger onto you. So what! You should be old enough to take this with compassion and even with humor.

Perhaps there is an important lesson that you can learn from your grandpa. If he is cynical and weird as you describe him, maybe you will determine not to be the same. Maybe he is setting a bad example for you without being aware of this. Good! If he has lead a life of being unhappy and negative, perhaps you will see the results and decide that you will live your life as a positive, compassionate, nurturing person.

I am sorry to be harsh with you. This is my reaction to a young person who seems to be filled with negatives. The world is certainly not perfect. It is not the world that Nicole or Bob would have made. But it is the only world we have. Instead of grumbling about it, let's try to spend our time and energy trying to fix it.

As a college student you obviously have talent. And you have youth and energy and time. How about using these precious gifts to do good deeds. You will become a more attractive person if you do.

With best wishes, Bob

Introspection

Dear Bob,

Chinese culture attaches great importance to balance of the universe, balance between Yin and Yang. What a wonderful world it would be if we could really enjoy a simple, natural and balanced life.

I am always busy, rushing to airports, attending parties and receptions, giving speeches, responding to questions, dashing around for appointments, keeping up with the news, and many more demands on my time and energy. I feel pushed around and have no control over my schedule, or my life. What I want most is a time for rest, books, my family and friends. How do you feel about this kind of life?

Chen

▲

Dear Chen,

Your letter raises a deep personal and philosophical dilemma that I have experienced all my life. This is the choice between detachment and involvement, between reflection and action, between contemplation and participation.

We want privacy, time for ourselves, time to look inward, time for family and friends. We want some quiet time with no external tugs, with no deadlines to meet. We want to separate ourselves from all the competition and rivalry of the outside world. We don't want to live in a society where someone else is telling us how to spend our time. We want peace and the freedom to decide how to spend our hours. We are tired of the alcohol, protocol, cholesterol world. We want to live and let live!

But there is another side of us. Many years ago I was told that while saints are engaged in introspection, the aggressive achievers run the world. Are we willing to step aside and let our lives be guided by others, by those aggressive achievers who are making decisions that will control our destiny?

We don't want to escape our responsibilities. We want to make a difference. We want to be out there fighting for what we believe, trying to make this world a better place to live and work in. We want to share our talents and our experience with others. We want to use our energy to tilt this planet toward goodness, fairness, mercy, and justice. We want to live and help live.

The choices we make are usually determined by our individual personalities and temperaments, and often by outside events. Some of us thrive on ambition. We want to be busy all the time. We want to have our lives remembered by what we have done. We want influence, status, and prestige. We are willing to give up precious time and energy to achieve recognition, to gain money and power. We want the excitement of . . . competing with the aggressive achievers. Sometimes it is a matter of opportunity. We are asked to participate in a life that places heavy demands on our time and energy. This life offers rewards to us in terms of prestige and even money and power. It is enticing to our egos. It gives us a feeling of achievement.

Another side of us yearns for the quieter life, perhaps a steady job with regulated hours and no competition. We want to leave the big social and political responsibilities to others. A popular expression tells us that "When the game is over, the king and the pawns go back into the same box." We question the rewards given to active achievers. The pressure to achieve and the financial and other rewards may not be enough to divert us from a quiet peaceful life where we have more control over our time and life styles.

There is no solution to this dilemma. We all have a responsibility to examine our lives and to make basic choices. You have reached an important goal of leading an active public life. Your time is valuable to others who are making heavy demands upon it. You are working successfully among the active achievers. You are making a contribution to the broader society. Now you question this pace. This could be a matter of fatigue, or of introspection. In either case you face a choice.

Having achieved success in a busy life, your next quest may be to find some way to balance this with a more contemplative, quieter existence. This is not easy. I wish you success in finding a balance between these two worlds. I also admire your ability to stand back and question your life. The famous philosopher, Socrates, told us that "the unexaminded life is not worth living." You are fortunate in being able to pause and examine.

Respectfully yours, Bob

About the Author

Dear Friends,

Many of our readers have asked questions concerning my private life. In my letters to you I try to avoid writing about myself. Now, on my ninetieth birthday, here is my response to your questions.

My life did not begin at eighty. But it took a sharp turn at eighty. The first eighty years were filled with action and movement. These included active participation in high school, college, and university studies, working with three famous New York State Governors, teaching economics and public administration at several universities, giving lectures on humor, advising foreign governments, being on numerous boards, commissions, and councils, and numerous other activities. It was a busy life.

At eighty, my life turned more inward. In the following five years I completed more than 50 poems for publication. I was also able to write about the same number of columns for two Chinese magazines, and to complete the book, *Adventures of the Mind*, also published in China.

One of the concerns of my life has been the contrast between mirrors and windows. When I look into the *mirror*, I see a life of constant privilege: good health, a stable childhood, caring parents and a caring brother, good education with advanced degrees, a loving wife for almost seventy years, two wonderful sons, many good friends, and several successful careers.

In my youth, during the 1930s and the 1940s, my ambition was to leave this world in a better condition than it was when I entered it. The second world war took almost four years of my life, but these were years of strength and hope. I was participating in a struggle to preserve freedom and dignity for all inhabitants of this planet. If we lost this struggle, we would all be speaking German or Japanese today and we would be living under terrible dictatorships based on fear and terror. We fought a good war and I was proud to be part of the winning side. This is what I see when I look into the mirror—a fortunate survivor of a world war, several successful careers, a happy marriage and healthy family, many faithful friends, and a long life.

In my youth it never occurred to me that I would still be alive in the year 2010. One reason for this longevity is modern medicine and the advances in vaccines, new medications and medical equipment, sanitation, and other forms of physical and mental hygiene. The average life span has almost doubled in some countries over this period. A number of inventions have made life easier for masses of people. We are able to travel farther and faster. There have been important gains in agriculture, transportation, education, construction, technology, and science. We know more and we understand more.

However, when I look out the *window* I see a different scene: massive poverty, disease and despair, world wide conflict, wasted environments, weapons of mass destruction, and enormous gaps between the rich and the poor.

Unfortunately, many of the scientific gains have not been shared with a large number of our people. We know more and we understand more, but this increased knowledge and understanding have often been used to exploit the natural and the human resources of our fragile planet. We have attacked our natural environment as if it were an enemy. We have added tons of pollution to our precious air and water while we watch the temperature of the planet drop to levels that can become dangerous. We allow millions of people to die from starvation every year while millions of others are facing problems of obesity. We have allowed the richest 500 individuals to have the same income as the world's poorest 420 million people. This is a privilege gap that relates to education and health and housing in addition to wealth and income. It is growing in most parts of the world. This is what I see when I look out the window.

What is the reason for this disparity between the mirror and the window? I believe it is our failure to define what we mean by "progress." We use this term loosely. Is it progress when we fill our jails, or when we achieve higher production records for automobiles and trucks? Is it progress when we spend more on armaments than on social services? Is it progress when we put persons on the moon, but our streets are not safe to walk on?

I ask you to consider what you would mean by progress on a planetary scale. And thank you for reading my life story and for understanding my troubled feelings between what I see in the mirror and what I see when I look out the window.

Respectfully yours,
Bob